Android Studio Cookbook

Design, debug, and test your apps using Android Studio

Mike van Drongelen

[PACKT] open source ✳
PUBLISHING   community experience distilled

BIRMINGHAM - MUMBAI

Android Studio Cookbook

First published: October 2015

Production reference: 1231015

Published by Packt Publishing Ltd.
Livery Place
35 Livery Street
Birmingham B3 2PB, UK.

ISBN 978-1-78528-618-6

www.packtpub.com

Cover image by Wim Wepster

Credits

Author

Mike van Drongelen

Reviewers

Aliaksandr Zhukovich

Ankit Garg

Nico Küchler

Acquisition Editor

Nikhil Karkal

Content Development Editor

Zeeyan Pinheiro

Technical Editor

Pranjali Mistry

Copy Editor

Neha Vyas

Project Coordinator

Suzanne Coutinho

Proofreader

Safis Editing

Indexer

Monica Ajmera Mehta

Graphics

Disha Haria

Production Coordinator

Arvindkumar Gupta

Cover Work

Arvindkumar Gupta

About the Author

Mike van Drongelen started developing software from the very first moment he had access to a computer. At the age of nine, he started programming in an obscure Basic variant. Currently, he works as a mobile solution consultant in the Netherlands. Besides this, he also runs his own start-up. He speaks English, Dutch, German, and a little French, but most of the time, he speaks Java, JavaScript, HTML, Objective C, Swift, C#, and ASP.NET. He develops Android, iOS, and .NET solutions for various customers and has some projects of his own. One of his projects is an e-learning solution called TeamSpot. Another one is Finiware, which is a company developing B2B specific solutions.

Creating better software using less code is what he is aiming for, which explains why he is interested in the lean start up methodology. In addition to this, he is interested in technology and topics such as continuous delivery, Test-driven development, and Behaviour Driven Development.

About these and other mobile related topics you can read his blog on `www.mikevandrongelen.info`. When he is not developing, he likes to go on trips on his motorbike or with his 2 CV.

You can find out more about his companies—Miker Works (`www.mikerworks.nl`), Finiware (`www.finiware.nl`), and TeamSpot (`www.teamspot.nl`)—on the Internet.

First of all, I would like to thank my wife, Lan Nguyen, for her support, and to Wim Wepster, who has been kind enough to create the front cover image in a material design style.

Also, I would like to thank the reviewers for their comments, and all the people at Packt Publishing who were involved in the creation of this book.

Finally, I would like to thank you for reading this book. I hope you enjoy reading it as much as did writing it.

About the Reviewers

Aliaksandr Zhukovich is a software enthusiast with a passion for technology and has more than four years of experience in professional software development. He has developed and designed software solutions for different areas. He graduated from College Business and Law and Baranovichi State University as a software developer.

He has already worked for multinational companies, such as Ericpol, as as Software developer and has worked with Java, C++, TTCN, and Android technologies. Currently, he works for TomTom as a mobile software engineer and works for a cross-platform Navigation Engine.

Ankit Garg works as a mobile engineer at AOL. He works in the Product Research and Development team and has about five years of experience in developing mobile applications. He is really passionate about making user-friendly mobile apps.

Nico Küchler lives in Berlin, Germany. He did an apprenticeship as a mathematical-technical software developer. He has worked for the gambling industry and as an online shop provider.

Since he last few years, he is working at Deutsche Post E-POST Development GmbH within the scope of Android app development.

He has also reviewed Testing and Securing Android Studio Applications for packt.

He is maintaining a project which provide a fast start with test driven Android app development `https://github.com/nenick/android-gradle-template`.

www.PacktPub.com

Support files, eBooks, discount offers, and more

For support files and downloads related to your book, please visit www.PacktPub.com.

Did you know that Packt offers eBook versions of every book published, with PDF and ePub files available? You can upgrade to the eBook version at www.PacktPub.com and as a print book customer, you are entitled to a discount on the eBook copy. Get in touch with us at service@packtpub.com for more details.

At www.PacktPub.com, you can also read a collection of free technical articles, sign up for a range of free newsletters and receive exclusive discounts and offers on Packt books and eBooks.

https://www2.packtpub.com/books/subscription/packtlib

Do you need instant solutions to your IT questions? PacktLib is Packt's online digital book library. Here, you can search, access, and read Packt's entire library of books.

Why subscribe?

- ▶ Fully searchable across every book published by Packt
- ▶ Copy and paste, print, and bookmark content
- ▶ On demand and accessible via a web browser

Free access for Packt account holders

If you have an account with Packt at www.PacktPub.com, you can use this to access PacktLib today and view 9 entirely free books. Simply use your login credentials for immediate access.

Table of Contents

Table of Contents

Preface

Android Studio is the best IDE for developing Android apps, and it is available for free to anyone who wants to develop professional Android apps.

Now with Android Studio, we have a stable and faster IDE, and it comes with a lot of cool stuff such as Gradle, better refactoring methods, and a much better layout editor. If you have used Eclipse, then you will love this IDE.

In short, Android Studio has really brought back the fun of mobile development, and in this book, we will see how.

What this book covers

Chapter 1, Welcome to Android Studio, demonstrates how to configure Android Studio and Genymotion, which is a really fast emulator.

Chapter 2, Applications with a Cloud-based Backend, explains how to use Parse to develop an app using a cloud-based backend in no time.

Chapter 3, Material Design, explains the concept of material design and how to implement it using RecycleViews, CardViews, and transitions.

Chapter 4, Android Wear, covers the Android Wear API and how to develop your own watch face or other apps running on a smart watch.

Chapter 5, Size Does Matter, demonstrates how using fragments and additional resources can help you to create an app that is able to run on a phone, phablet, tablet, or even on TV. On the fly, we will connect to the YouTube API to make the recipes more fun.

Chapter 6, Capture and Share, is an in-depth tutorial about capturing and previewing images using the new Camera2 API, in particular. It also tells you how to share a captured image on Facebook.

Chapter 7, Content Providers and Observers, explains how you can benefit from using content providers to display and observe persisting data.

Chapter 8, Improving Quality, elaborates on applying patterns, unit testing, and code analysis tools.

Chapter 9, Improving Performance, covers how the Device Monitor can be used to optimize your apps' memory management and how the developer options on your phone can be used to detect overdraw and other performance issues.

Chapter 10, Beta Testing Your Apps, guides you through some of the final steps such as using build variants (types and flavors) and beta distribution on the Google Play Store. In addition to this, it covers how the run time permissions that come with Android Marshmallow (6.0) differ from the install permissions.

What you need for this book

For this book, you need to download and set up Android Studio and the latest SDKs. Android Studio is free and is available for Windows, OSX, and Linux.

Having at least one phone, phablet, or tablet is strongly recommended, but in *Chapter 1, Welcome to Android Studio* we will introduce you to Genymotion, a really fast emulator, which you can use instead of a real device in most cases.

Finally, for some recipes, you need to have a Google developer account. If you do not have one yet, I suggest that you get one as soon as possible. After all, you will need one in order to be able to get your app into the Play Store.

Who this book is for

This book is for anyone who is already familiar with the Java syntax and perhaps has already developed some Android apps, for example, using the Eclipse IDE.

This book explains the concepts of Android development using Android Studio in particular. To demonstrate these concepts, real-world recipes are provided. And, by real-world apps, I mean apps that do connect to a backend and communicate with Google Play services or Facebook and so on.

Sections

In this book, you will find several headings that appear frequently (Getting ready, How to do it, How it works, There's more, and See also).

To give clear instructions on how to complete a recipe, we use these sections as follows:

Getting ready

This section tells you what to expect in the recipe, and describes how to set up any software or any preliminary settings required for the recipe.

How to do it...

This section contains the steps required to follow the recipe.

How it works...

This section usually consists of a detailed explanation of what happened in the previous section.

There's more...

This section consists of additional information about the recipe in order to make the reader more knowledgeable about the recipe.

See also

This section provides helpful links to other useful information for the recipe.

Conventions

All screenshots, shortcuts and other elements that are specific for Android Studio are based on Android Studio for OSX.

The main reason that OSX is being used is because it allows us to develop apps for both Android and iOS on the same machine. Other than that there is no reason to choose a particular OS other than your personal (or companies) preferences.

While the screenshots are based on Android Studio for OSX it is not too difficult for you to figure things out in case your OS is Windows or Linux.

Where needed the short cuts for Windows are mentioned as well.

In this book, you will find a number of text styles that distinguish between different kinds of information. Here are some examples of these styles and an explanation of their meaning.

Code words in text, database table names, folder names, filenames, file extensions, pathnames, dummy URLs, user input, and Twitter handles are shown as follows: "We can include other contexts through the use of the include directive."

A block of code is set as follows:

```
public void onSectionAttached(int number) {
    switch (number) {
        case 0:
            mTitle = getString(
              R.string.title_section_daily_notes);
            break;

        case 1:
            mTitle = getString(
              R.string.title_section_note_list);
            break;
    }
}
```

New terms and **important words** are shown in bold. Words that you see on the screen, for example, in menus or dialog boxes, appear in the text like this: "Clicking the **Next** button moves you to the next screen."

Warnings or important notes appear in a box like this.

Tips and tricks appear like this.

Reader feedback

Feedback from our readers is always welcome. Let us know what you think about this book—what you liked or may have disliked. Reader feedback is important for us to develop titles that you really get the most out of.

To send us general feedback, simply send an e-mail to feedback@packtpub.com, and mention the book title via the subject of your message.

If there is a topic that you have expertise in and you are interested in either writing or contributing to a book, see our author guide on www.packtpub.com/authors.

Customer support

Now that you are the proud owner of a Packt book, we have a number of things to help you to get the most from your purchase.

Downloading the example code

You can download the example code files for all Packt books you have purchased from your account at http://www.packtpub.com. If you purchased this book elsewhere, you can visit http://www.packtpub.com/support and register to have the files e-mailed directly to you.

Downloading the color images of this book

We also provide you with a PDF file that has color images of the screenshots/diagrams used in this book. The color images will help you better understand the changes in the output. You can download this file from https://www.packtpub.com/sites/default/files/downloads/B04299_ColoredImages.pdf.

Errata

Although we have taken every care to ensure the accuracy of our content, mistakes do happen. If you find a mistake in one of our books—maybe a mistake in the text or the code—we would be grateful if you would report this to us. By doing so, you can save other readers from frustration and help us improve subsequent versions of this book. If you find any errata, please report them by visiting http://www.packtpub.com/submit-errata, selecting your book, clicking on the **errata submission form** link, and entering the details of your errata. Once your errata are verified, your submission will be accepted and the errata will be uploaded on our website, or added to any list of existing errata, under the Errata section of that title. Any existing errata can be viewed by selecting your title from http://www.packtpub.com/support.

Piracy

Piracy of copyright material on the Internet is an ongoing problem across all media. At Packt, we take the protection of our copyright and licenses very seriously. If you come across any illegal copies of our works, in any form, on the Internet, please provide us with the location address or website name immediately so that we can pursue a remedy.

Please contact us at `copyright@packtpub.com` with a link to the suspected pirated material.

We appreciate your help in protecting our authors, and our ability to bring you valuable content.

Questions

You can contact us at `questions@packtpub.com` if you are having a problem with any aspect of the book, and we will do our best to address it.

1
Welcome to Android Studio

In this chapter, we will cover some basic tasks related to Android Studio. While reading this and the other chapters, you will learn how to use Android Studio efficiently.

In this chapter, you will learn the following recipes:

- Creating your first app called `Hello Android Studio`.
- The use of Gradle build scripts
- Testing your app with an emulator called Genymotion
- Refactoring your code

Introduction

This chapter is an introduction to Android Studio and provides a helicopter view of the different tools that come with this **Integrated Development Environment (IDE)**. In addition to this, some other important tools will be discussed here, such as Genymotion, the emulator that I highly recommend you to use to test your app on different kinds of devices.

Using Android Studio, you can create any app you like. Apps for phones, phablets, tablets, watches and other wearables, Google Glass, TV apps, and even auto apps.

If you already have mobile programming experience or even have worked with Android apps and Eclipse before and you want to discover how to create apps that take pictures, play media, work on any device, connect to a cloud, or anything else that you can think of, then this book is for you!

All recipes described in this book are based on Android Studio for Mac; however, it is not a problem at all if you are using Android Studio for Windows or Linux instead. The terminology is the same for all platforms. Just the screenshots provided with each recipe may look a little bit different, but I am pretty sure you can figure that out with a little effort. If there are any significant differences for Windows, I will let you know.

Reasons why we should use Android Studio

Android Studio is the recommended IDE to develop Android apps and is available for free for anyone who develops professional Android apps. Android Studio is based on the JetBrains IntelliJ IDEA software, which might explain why even the preview and beta versions of Android studio were already better than Eclipse and why many Android developers were using it as their IDE from the beginning.

The first stable build of Android Studio was released in December 2014 and has replaced Eclipse (with Android Development Tools) as the primary IDE for Android development. Now, with Android Studio, we do not just have a more stable and faster IDE, but it also comes with cool stuff such as Gradle, better refactoring methods, and a much better layout editor to name just a few of them.

Okay, I still have some weird issues every now and then (I guess that is what life as a mobile developer is all about sometimes) but I certainly do not feel the frustration that I had felt when I was working with Eclipse. If you are using Eclipse for plain Java development, it is just fine I guess; however, it does not play nicely with Android. If you have been using IntelliJ IDEA for Java development tasks before, then Android Studio will look pretty familiar to you.

Android Studio really brought back the fun of mobile development. If you are using Eclipse currently, then you should switch to Android Studio instantly! To see it for yourself, get it from `https://developer.android.com/sdk/index.html` and start building cool apps using Android Studio right away.

Fragmentation

What has remained is the fragmentation challenge that you need to deal with when it comes to Android development. There are many devices running on many Android flavors and versions.

There are a lot of Android versions, resulting in fragmentation. Because of this, you cannot expect that all devices will run on the latest Android version. In fact, most do not. Many devices still run on Android 4.x (or even older versions), for example.

Here, you can see a table with all the relevant Android versions and distribution numbers. The numbers in this table indicate that if you decide to support Android 4.0 and later releases, you will reach 88.7 percent of all Android users. In this example, the numbers for Q2 2015 are shown, which explains why **Android Marshmallow (6.0)** is not being listed here. If you create a new project in Android Studio, you can get the actual numbers by clicking on a **Help me Choose** link in the **Create New project** wizard dialog, as we will find out in the next chapters.

Let's have a look at the following screenshot which describes the cumulative distribution of different Android platform version along with their API level:

ANDROID PLATFORM VERSION	API LEVEL	CUMULATIVE DISTRIBUTION
2.2 Froyo	8	99,7%
2.3 Gingerbread	10	94,0%
4.0 Ice Cream Sandwich	15	88,7%
4.1 Jelly Bean	16	73,1%
4.2 Jelly Bean	17	55,0%
4.3 Jelly Bean	18	49,5%
4.4 KitKat	19	9,7%
5.0 Lollipop	21	

In addition to software fragmentation, there is also a lot of hardware fragmentation that you should be aware of. Writing an Android app is not that hard but writing an app that functions well on any Android device actually is.

A good app should be able to run on as many different devices as possible. For example, think of an app that takes pictures. Android devices do have a camera or multiple ones or no camera at all. Depending on other functionalities that your app provides, you might need to worry about other things as well, such as whether a device is able to record sound or not.

I can imagine you want to reach an audience as large as possible so you should always ask yourself which of your app feature demands will or will not have to be mandatory. If a device does not have a camera, the user might not be able to take pictures, but should that really be a reason for not allowing the user to use the app at all?

The introduction of runtime permissions in Android Marshmallow (6.0) makes it even more important for you to provide some kind of a fallback functionality in your app. At least you need to explain why a particular functionality is not available in your app. For example, the user device does not support it or the user did not gave permission for it.

This book is going to help you deal with Android fragmentation and other issues.

Creating your first app called Hello Android Studio

After downloading Android Studio, install it and go through the setup wizards. The wizard checks for some requirements, whether the **Java Development Kit** (**JDK**) is available, and other important elements that the installation wizards guide you through.

Once the installation is complete, it is time to develop your first Android app using Android Studio, just to check whether everything has been installed correctly and works the way it should. It probably will be no surprise that this is where the Hello Android Studio recipe comes in.

Getting ready

To go through this recipe, you will need a running Android Studio IDE, an Android **Software Development Kit** (**SDK**), and an Android device. No other prerequisites are required.

How to do it...

Let's create our first Android app using Android Studio to check whether everything works fine with the help of the following steps:

1. Start Android Studio. The **Welcome to Android Studio** dialog will be shown to you after a few seconds.

2. Select the **Start a new Android Studio project** option. Then, the **Configure your new project** dialog appears.

3. For **Application name**, enter `HelloAndroidStudio`; and for the **Company domain** field, enter `packtpub.com` (or use the domain name of your own company if you prefer to do so).

4. Package names such as `packtpub.com` and `helloandroidstudio` are suggested and updated while you type. If you wish, you can edit the **Project location** before you click on the **Next** button.

5. In the **Target Android Devices** dialog box, check the **Phone and Tablet** option. Leave the other options unchecked. We will create some of those other interesting targets, such as an Android Wear app, later. For the **Minimum SDK**, choose **API 14**. If that one is not (yet) available, click on any of the other available SDKs. We will install more SDKs later. Click on the **Next** button to continue.

6. In the next dialog box, **Add an activity to Mobile**, choose the **Blank Activity** option and click on the **Next** button.

7. The final dialog **Customize the activity** will be displayed after this. Leave all the values the way they are and click on the **Finish** button.

8. Android Studio is now going to create this new app for you. After a while, the project view, a **MainActivity** class, and an **activity_main.xml** layout are displayed. If you change the perspective of the project view on the left-hand side of your Android Studio by clicking on the button, that displays the little green Android guy and the text that reads **Android**, from **Android** to **Project**, the layout will look a little bit more like you are used to, that is, if you have used Eclipse before.

9. Double-click on the **app** folder to expand it. You will notice a file called the `build.gradle` file (note that this file also exists on the root level).

10. Double-click on the `build.gradle` file to open it and have a look at the values for `compileSdkVersion`, `minSdkVersion`, and `targetSdkVersion`. By default, the `compileSdkVersion` value is always related to the latest (available) SDK. The value for `minSdkVersion` is the one that you have chosen in the **Target Android devices** dialog box.

> If you want, use a different SDK to compile against; you must change the value for `compileSdkVersion`. The version you choose might need to be installed first. If you are happy with the current configuration, go to step 14 right away.

11. If you want to check which SDKs are installed, go the **Tools** option from the main menu and choose **Android** from the **SDK Manager** submenu.

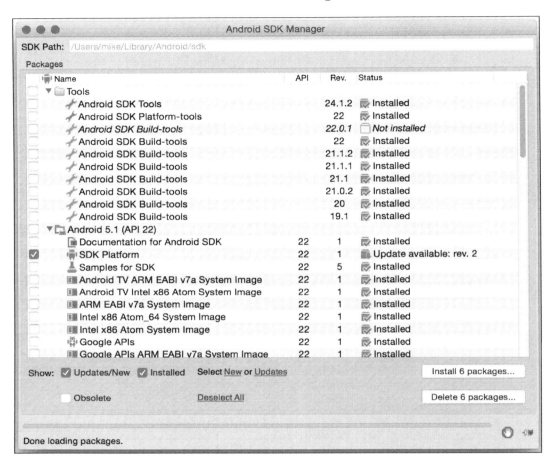

12. The **Android SDK Manager** dialog box displays which SDKs are installed. If you need to install a different SDK, you can check the elements you need and click on the **Install n packages...** button.

13. After installing the SDKs that you need and having configured your `build.gradle` file, you can now run your app.

14. If you are using a physical device for Android development, you need to unlock the developer options first. On your device, start the **Settings** app and go to the **Device info** option. (This option may be on the **General** tab or section or at another place, depending on the version and flavor of Android that your device is running on).

If you do not have a real device, I strongly recommend you get one as soon as possible. To get started, you can use an emulator for now. You can use the emulator that comes with the Android SDK or you can read the recipe about Genymotion first to find out how to use emulated devices.

15. In the **Device Info** view, scroll all the way down until you see the **Build number** option. Now, click seven (7) times on **Build number** to unlock (enable) the developer mode. (No, this is not a joke). You now have the developer's menu unlocked.

 On older Android versions (below 4.2), this step may be skipped, or if the developer options are already available as a menu item in the settings app, this step may be skipped.

16. Now that you have got a new option in your **Settings** app, called **Developer options**, click on it and have a look at it. It is important that you enable the **USB debugging** option within this menu. In addition, you might want to enable or disable some of the other options.

17. Connect your device and run your app from Android Studio by clicking on the green triangle next to the drop-down box that reads the app. Or, choose the **Run...** option from the **Run** menu. Then, the **Choose Device** dialog box appears. Your device should now appear in the list of the **Choose a running device** option. (If your device does not appear in the list, reconnect your device).

18. Click on the **OK** button. (For Windows, before you are able to connect your device, it is often necessary to install a driver first.)

19. On your device, a dialog box may pop up, requiring you to accept the finger print. Choose **Allow** in order to continue.

The app is now being deployed on your device. If everything goes well, your new app is now shown on your device that says **Hello world!** Hurrah! I admit this is not really a very exciting app, but at least we know now that Android Studio and your device have been configured correctly.

How it works...

Android Studio will take care of the basic parts of your app setup. All you need to do is choose the target and minimal SDK for your app. Using the API level 14 (Android 4.0) is currently the best option, as this will allow your app to run on most Android devices.

The app will be compiled against the chosen (compile) SDK by Android Studio.

The app will be copied to your device. Having the **USB debugging** option enabled will help you troubleshoot any issues, as we will find out later.

The use of Gradle build scripts

Android Studio uses Gradle build scripts. It is a project automation tool and uses a **Domain-specific Language** (**DSL**) instead of the more common XML form to create the configuration of a project.

Projects come with a top-level build file and a build file for each module. These files are called `build.gradle`. Most of the time, it is only the build file for the app module that needs your attention.

 You may note that some properties that you could find in the Android manifest file previously, such as the target SDK and versioning properties, are now defined in a build file and should reside in the build file only.

A typical `build.gradle` file may look like this:

```
applylugin: 'com.android.application'
android {
  compileSdkVersion 21
  buildToolsVersion "21.0.0"
  defaultConfig {
  minSdkVersion 8
  targetSdkVersion 21
  versionCode 1
  versionName "0.1"
  }
}
dependencies {
  compile fileTree(dir: 'libs', include: ['*.jar'])
}
```

The Gradle build system is not something that you need to worry too much about right now. In later recipes, we will see what the real power of it will be. The system is also designed to support complex scenarios that may be faced while creating Android applications, such as handling customized versions of the same app for various customers (build flavors) or creating multiple APK files for different device types or different Android OS versions.

For now, it is ok just to know that this is the place where we will define `compileSdkVersion`, `targetSdkVersion`, and `minSdkVersion`, just like we did in the manifest file previously in case you have been using Eclipse.

Also, this is the place where we define `versionCode` and `versionName`, which reflect the version of your app that is useful if someone is going to update the app you wrote.

Another interesting key element of the Gradle functionality is that of dependencies. Dependencies can be local or remote libraries and JAR files. The project depends on them in order to be able to compile and run. In the `build.gradle` file that you will find in the previous folder the `app` folder you will find the defined repository in which the libraries reside. `jCenter` is the default repository.

If for example you wish to add the `Parse` functionality, which is something that we will do in the recipes found in the next chapter, the following dependency declaration will add the local Parse library to your project:

```
dependencies {
    compile fileTree(dir: 'libs', include: 'Parse-*.jar')
    compile project(':Parse-1.9.1')
}
```

Using external libraries has become much easier. For example, if you want to add `UniversalImageLoader`, a well-known library to load images from the Internet, or if you want to use the functionality from the `Gson` library, which basically is an object wrapper for JSON data, to your app, the following dependency declaration will make these libraries available to the project:

```
dependencies {
compile 'com.google.code.gson:gson:2.3+'
compile 'com.nostra13.universalimageloader:universal-image-
loader:1.9.3'
}
```

There's more...

Some other Gradle concepts will be explained in the recipes of the next chapters. Gradle is a topic that one could write a book about on, and you can find many interesting in-depth tutorials on the Internet if you would like to know more about it.

See also

▶ For more information about Gradle build scripts, refer to *Chapter 2, Applications with a Cloud-based Backend*

Testing your app with an emulator called Genymotion

The best way to test your app is by using a real device. The Android emulator is pretty slow and does not provide you with all the features that come with a real device, such as a camera and all kinds of sensors.

I can image that you do have just one or perhaps a few devices. With thousands of Android devices being available and many brands and models that run on a customized (for example, the Samsung devices) or a plain (like the Nexus devices) flavor of the Android OS and on any Android version that you can think of, testing on real devices only would become pretty expensive.

If, for example, you are creating an app that should run well on Android 2.3, Android 4.x, and Android 5.x, using emulated devices can be handy. Unfortunately, the default emulator is terribly slow. It takes ages to start Android on the emulator, and debugging can be very slow on it as well. To make the emulator a little bit faster, you could try to install **Hardware Accelerated Execution Manager** (**HAXM**). There are some topics on the Internet that tell you how to do this; however, there is a much better solution, Genymotion.

Genymotion is a real, fast, and easy-to-use emulator and comes with many real-world device configurations. You can read more about Genymotion on its website at `www.genymotion.com`. It is available as a free or paid solution. The free one will be all right to start with.

Getting ready

Make sure you have Internet access and sufficient space on your hard drive. We will need to download both VirtualBox and Genymotion. After this, you are ready to create your first virtual device. Let the magic begin.

How to do it...

Let's install Genymotion to prepare Android Studio to work with smoothly running emulated devices:

1. Both Oracle's VirtualBox and the Genymotion app need to be installed. This is because Genymotion virtualizes various Android operating systems using the virtualization techniques of **Oracle Virtual Machine** (**VM**) VirtualBox in the background. If you do not already have Oracle VM VirtualBox installed on your computer (or if you have a version of VirtualBox that is below 4.1.1 which is not compatible with Genymotion), you need to install it first.

    Download VirtualBox for OS X hosts (or for Windows) from the VirtualBox download page at `https://www.virtualbox.org/wiki/Downloads`.

    Install VirtualBox, and after that, reboot your computer.

    Download Genymotion from its web page at `https://www.genymotion.com/#!/download`.

2. Now, open and install the downloaded file.

3. Run Genymotion. A dialog box then asks you whether you want to create a new device. Click on the **Yes** button to do so. Later, you can create additional devices by clicking on the + (plus) button on the main screen.

4. Select the Android OS version from the drop-down list on the left-hand side of dialog box.

5. Select a virtual device (brand and model) from the drop-down list on the center and click on the **Next** button.

6. Name your device. It's recommended that you include both the device and the OS version in your device name so what you are testing on can be easily recognized when you want to use it later.

7. Click on the **Next** button to confirm the name. Your virtual device will be created, and it will appear in the list on the main screen of Genymotion. Create as many virtual devices as you need.

8. To run a virtual device, select it and click on the **Play** button. It will launch the Genymotion emulator so that you can use it together with Android Studio. When it is launched, you can unlock the device so that it is ready to use.

9. If you hit the **Run** button in Android Studio again, you will notice that the running virtual device is shown in the list of available devices in the **Choose Device** dialog box. Just click on the **OK** button to let the magic begin. Your Android app will be launched on the emulator.

And it is running fast and smooth! Pretty cool, isn't it?

The following is an example of the main screen of Genymotion listing a couple of virtual devices that have been created:

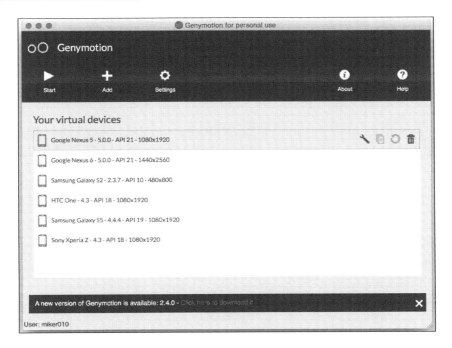

There's more...

Genymotion comes with emulated front and/or backend cameras, depending on the chosen configuration. To enable them, click on the camera icon. A new dialog box appears in which you can change the slider to **On** and choose a real camera for the front and backend camera of your virtual device.

After selecting a camera, you can close the dialog box. A green checkbox will now appear next to the Camera button. Now, whenever an app needs to use a camera, it will use the selected camera, which in my case is the webcam on the laptop. To check whether this is working, choose the Camera app on the virtual device.

The paid version of Genymotion has additional features available, including emulated sensors such as GPS and accelerometers. If you like, you can check out the differences at `https://www.genymotion.com/#!/store`.

Remember that although using virtual devices for testing purposes works really great with Genymotion, it is important to always test it on multiple real devices. Some issues, in particular the ones that are related to memory management that we will see later in this book, are easy to reproduce on real devices, but may be somewhat harder to reproduce on virtual devices.

In addition to this, real devices are much more pixel perfect and some issues may appear only on a particular device so when it comes to see how the artwork looks, you are going to need a couple of them.

By the time your app is nearly complete, you might be interested in the (paid) services from Testdroid, a cloud-based service that allows to run (automated) tests on many real devices. Visit `www.testdroid.com` to learn more about this great service!

The following screenshot provides an example of the Hello Android Studio app running on a virtual Nexus 5 device using Genymotion:

Refactoring your code

Good software engineers refactor their work continuously. Names of methods and members should always indicate what they are doing. Since business requirements often change during the development process, in particular when agile methodologies come in, so do your apps.

If you choose the right names and stick to the rule that the length of methods must be limited to, well let's say, scrolling one page at most to view the whole method, often you do not need many comments to explain what your code is doing. If it is hard to come up with a good name for a particular method, then it is probably doing too much.

Since changing names could be scary, as it could break your code, developers often choose not to do so. Or, they decide to do it later. You save yourself a few minutes by doing so in advance. Your code could be hard to understand if some one else has a look at your code or if you have a look at your code one year later. Going through the code to find out what a method does can be very time consuming. A descriptive name for your method can solve this.

The good news is that using Android Studio, refactoring is painless and pretty easy. Just highlight the name of a member or method, right-click on it, and pick the **Refactor** item from the context menu that pops up.

In the **Refactor** submenu that appears when you choose the **Refactor** item, you will find many interesting options. The one option that you will use here and which you will be using the most is the **Rename...** option.

How to do it...

The following steps describe how to rename a method in the Refactor submenu:

1. Highlight the name of the method you would like to rename.

2. From the context menu, choose **Refactor**.

3. From the submenu, choose **Rename** (or use the shortcut *Shift + F6*).

4. Now, you can rename your method or member in place and apply the changes by hitting the *Enter* button. Android Studio provides you with some suggestions that you can accept or you can type the name you want.

 If you repeat step 2 and 3, a dialog box appears in which you can edit the name. (Or use the shortcut *Shift + F6* twice).

5. Click on the **Preview** button to see what the effect of the renaming will be.

6. At the bottom of your screen, a new view appears, which shows you the impact of the renaming in each file (class, resource, or otherwise).

7. Click on the **Do refactor** button in that view to apply all the changes.

The following screenshot shows an example of an in-place refactoring (renaming).

```
private CloudRepository mRepository;
                        cloudRepository
public static ProjectFr repository                Activity)
{                        mRepository
    ProjectFragment fra  mrepository
    fragment.mPickForNe Press ⇧F6 to show dialog with more options
    return fragment;
}

public ProjectFragment()
{


}
```

How it works...

Android Studio will take care of renaming a method or member and any references to it everywhere in the project. This includes Java classes, layouts, drawables, and anything else that you can think of.

There are many other interesting options available from the **Refactor** menu that you can use. Some of them will be discussed in the next chapters in the recipes where they will come in handy.

Now, let's move on to the next chapter and build a real app, shall we?

See also

▶ For more information about refactoring code, refer to *Chapter 8, Improving quality.*

2
Applications with a Cloud-based Backend

This chapter will teach you how to build an app that does not need a backend of its own but uses a cloud-based solution instead.

In this chapter, you will learn the following recipes:

- ▶ Setting up Parse
- ▶ Consuming data from the cloud
- ▶ Submitting data to the cloud

Introduction

Many applications require a backend solution, allowing users to communicate with a server or with each other like in social apps, for example, and which application is not social today? You can also think of a business app, for example, one for logistic purposes.

Sure, we can write our own API, host it somewhere, and write some Android code to communicate with it, including querying, caching, and all other functionalities that our application needs to support. Unfortunately, developing all this could be a very time-consuming process, and since this is often the most valuable asset, there must be another way to do this.

The good news is that you do not have to do all these things yourself. There are a couple of ready-made mobile backend solutions available on the Internet, such as QuickBlox, Firebase, Google App Engine, and Parse to mention just a few of the most well-known ones.

Each of these solutions do particular things well; although, one solution will be more suitable than another. For example, take QuickBlox, which provides the quickest way to set things up, but at a price. It also is not as flexible as the other options. Firebase, recently acquired by Google, is a very great solution in particular if you need real-time support; for example, for a chat app. Parse, acquired by Facebook, has no real-time options but is more flexible and has some interesting third-party integrations to offer.

There are, of course, other considerations when choosing a particular solution. The parties (Facebook and Google) that provide this kind of solutions might have access to the data that you store in the cloud, including your user base, which is not necessarily a bad thing right away, but it may have an impact on the strategy that you choose. Also, think about issues such as scalability and data lock-in that are both luxury problems, but nevertheless could become issues when your app becomes more popular.

Parse is my favourite as it currently is the most flexible solution for most purposes. It has no data lock-in (all data is exportable), but it is scalable (if you choose a paid plan instead of the free one), it is available for all relevant mobile platforms, and it even allows us to create cloud modules (methods that run in the cloud that could be scheduled on a regular base and/or that could be approached by your application). From all the available popular services, this one provides the easiest way to attach a backend to a mobile app.

 In future this might change, in particular for Android developers, if the Google App Engine (which by the way can be used for iOS apps as well) integration with Android Studio is further improved. You can find the **Deploy Module to App Engine** option in the **Build** menu already.

Setting up Parse

Think of a scenario that goes like this: at a central point, orders are being collected and will be prepared for transport. Goods need to be delivered and customers need to sign in the app once they receive the goods that they have ordered. Each driver has a mobile device and an app to support this process digitally.

This is the process for which we will provide the next three recipes and we will be using Parse for it, as it is the most suitable backend for the solution that we are going to create.

The upcoming recipe describes how to set up Parse, how to consume data from Parse into your Android app, and how to send data, such as a signature, from the app to Parse.

Getting ready

To go through this recipe, you will need Android Studio up and running and Internet access. That's all folks.

How to do it...

Let's create an app that connects to a Parse backend first so that we have a fundament on which we can build our app. Let's name our app `CloudOrder`. The further steps are as follows:

1. Start Android Studio and start a new Android Studio Project. Name your application `CloudOrder` and enter `packtpub.com` for the **Company Domain** field or any other name that suits you or your company best. Then, click on the Next button.

2. Select the **Phone and Tablet** option and optionally change the **minimum SDK** field. In my case, this will be API 14 (Android 4.x), which at the time of writing is the best choice to both reach an audience as large as possible and to benefit from the SDK functionality that we need. Make sure you will be targeting at least API level 9 as Parse does not support lower levels than this one. Click on the **Next** button to continue.

3. Next, select **Blank activity** and click on the **Next** button. On the next page, just click on the **Finish** button. Your new project will be set up by Android Studio.

4. Now, let's go to `www.parse.com` to create a new account and an app. Sign up with `www.Parse.com`. Enter your name, e-mail address, and chosen password, and then click on the **Sign up** button.

5. The next page on `www.Parse.com` is the **Get Started** page. Enter `CloudOrder` or something similar in the field displaying the hint about your app name. Pick a value for **Company type** that suits your situation best and depending on the chosen value, complete any of the other fields. Once this is done, hit the **Start using Parse** button. Select **Data** as the product you want to start using. Choose **Mobile** as your environment. Next, select a platform. Choose **Android**, and in the next view, choose the **Native (Java)** option.

6. Choose the **Existing project** option. We are creating a new project; however, to know what is going on here, we will do the following things ourselves.

7. Now, download the SDK. While downloading, switch to Android Studio and change the project view perspective from **Android** to **Project**. Then, expand the `app` folder. Note that one of the underlying folders is called `libs`.

8. Drag and drop the `Parse-x.x.x.jar` file (where `x.x.x` indicates the version number) into the `libs` folder in Android Studio. If the **Non-Project Files Access** dialog box appears, just click on the **OK** button. When you do this, `Parse-x.x.x.jar` will appear under the `libs` folder.

9. As we saw in *Chapter 1, Welcome to Android Studio,* we need to tell Gradle about this Parse library. Open the `build.gradle` file in the `apps` folder by double-clicking on it. In the dependencies section, we need to add two lines, so it will look like as shown in the following example. Just after the two lines that are already in there, add the dependencies for both the `bolts` and `parse` libraries:

```
dependencies {
    compile 'com.android.support:appcompat-v7:22.0.0'
    compile 'com.parse.bolts:bolts-android:1.+'
    compile fileTree(dir: 'libs', include: 'Parse-*.jar')
}
```

> Instead of using the local JAR file, as described through step 6 to 8, we could also use a dependency like this:
>
> ```
> dependencies {
> ...
>     compile 'com.parse:android:1.8.2'
> }
> ```

10. In the `AndroidManifest.xml` file, add permissions needed to access the Internet. The `Manifest` file will reside in the `/app/src/main` folder. Double-click on it to open it. Add the permissions for both the Internet and to access the network state, as shown in the following example. Also, define the name for the `package name` + `CloudOrderApplication` application:

```
<?xml version="1.0" encoding="utf-8"?>
<manifest xmlns:android="http://schemas.android.com/apk/res/
android"
    package="com.packtpub.cloudorder" >
    <uses-permission android:name="android.permission.INTERNET" />
    <uses-permission android:name= "android.permission.ACCESS_
NETWORK_STATE" />
<application
    android:name="com.packtpub.cloudorder.CloudOrderApplication"
```

11. Select and expand the `src/main/java/com.packt.cloudorder` folder. Right-click on this folder. In the context menu that pops up, choose **New**, and in the submenu, choose **Java Class**. In the dialog box that will be shown, enter `CloudOrderApplication` as the content for the **Name** field. Then, click on the **OK** button.

12. Make the new class a descendant of the `Application` class and override the `onCreate` method. In the `onCreate` method, right after `super.OnCreate()`, add the initialization for Parse, as indicated by Parse using the following code:

```
Parse.initialize(this, "your application Id", "your client Id");
```

13. Android Studio is not happy yet. You will notice that the Parse part in your code is highlighted in red in the Android Studio IDE. This is because your app is not aware of this class. Any time you change a `gradle` file, your project needs to be synchronized. To do so, click on the button with the tooltip that reads **Sync project with Gradle Files**. You will find this on the navigation bar. Alternatively, you may also click on the **Sync Now** link.

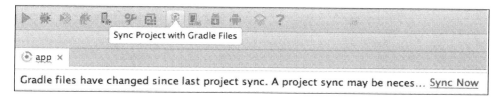

14. After this synchronization, Android Studio will have a clue about the Parse class, but you still need to add an import clause for that. If you hover over the part of your code that reads `Parse`, you will notice that Android Studio suggests that this probably refers to `com.parse.Parse`. Press *Alt + Enter* to accept this suggestion or just add the `import com.parse.Parse` line yourself. Finally, your class will look like this:

```
package com.packt.cloudorder;
import android.app.Application;
import com.parse.Parse;
public class CloudOrderApplication extends Application{
    @Override
    public void onCreate(){
        super.onCreate();
        Parse.enableLocalDatastore(this);
        Parse.initialize(this, "your application Id", "your client Id");
    }
}
```

15. We are almost done configuring our Parse-based app. Open the `MainActivity` file and add the following lines to your `onCreate` method:

```
ParseObject testObject = new ParseObject("CloudOrder");
testObject.put("customer", "Packt Publishing Ltd");
testObject.saveInBackground();
```

16. Don't forget to add the appropriate import statement. Run your app. If everything is set up successfully, a new object of the `CloudOrder` class is sent to Parse and created at Parse.

17. On the parse web page, click on the **Core** button at the top of the navigation bar. Have a look at the **Data** section on the left-hand side of web page. **CloudOrder** should appear there, and if you click on it, you will see the entry (row), containing the properties (fields) that you just sent.

    This is what the data section at www.Parse.com looks like:

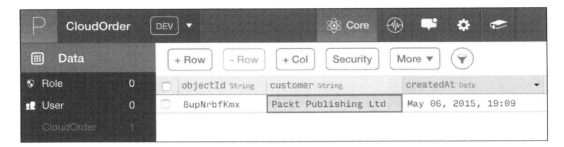

If this test succeeds, remove the three lines that you have added to the onCreate method of MainActivity as we no longer need them.

Well done! You have just created your first Parse app! Let's move on and see how to extend the CloudOrder app!

How it works...

The Parse SDK will take care of retrieving or sending data. Using the ParseObject class, Query and other Parse classes' all data communication takes place automatically.

There's more...

At www.parse.com, you will find additional information about caching policies, saving data to the cloud, and other interesting features.

Consuming data from the cloud

We have our Parse-based app up and running. Now, let's see how we can get the orders from Parse into our app and display them in a list.

Getting ready

To go through this recipe, you will need to have the previous recipe up and running, Internet access, and some coffee, although I must admit that last one is not strictly necessary. Tea will be just as fine.

How to do it...

Let's see how we can extend our `CloudOrder` app by consuming orders from the Parse backend and display them using a list view with the help of the following steps:

1. In the last step in the *Setting up Parse* recipe, we were looking at the newly created Parse entity and the data in there. Entities can be created or extended on the fly from your app like we did, but we can also define columns and add data here on the webpage. Click on the **+Col** button to add a new column to the `CargoOrder` entity.

2. In the modal, display **Add a column**, choose **String** from **Select a type**, and name the new column `address`. Then, click on the **Create Column** button. The new column will be added to the row that is already available (you might need to scroll to the right to see this.)

3. Add another column. From the type drop down box, choose **File** and name this field as `signature`. And finally, add a last column with the **Number** type and the `Status` name. We now have three new custom columns for each **CargoOrder** row.

4. Click on the **address** column and enter an address for it; for example, let's say that the delivery address for the order should be `1600 Amphitheatre Pkwy, Mountain View, CA 94043, United States` (it's where you can find the Google headquarters, but you can of course enter any address you like here).

5. Click on the **+Row** button to create a new **Cargo Order** row and enter some other values for the **customer** and **address** fields. Repeat this a couple of times to make sure that we have some data to consume in our app.

6. To retrieve rows from the **CargoOrder** entry, we first need to create a model that represents the orders. Create a new class at the location where your `MainActivity` and `CloudOrderApplication` classes reside. Right-click on the package name and select **New** and **Java Class**. Name your new class `CloudOrder` and hit the **OK** button. Make your model a descendant of the `ParseObject` class and indicate to which entity this class is mapping. Your class should look like this:

```
package com.packt.cloudorder;
import com.parse.ParseClassName;
import com.parse.ParseObject;
@ParseClassName("CloudOrder")
public class CloudOrder extends ParseObject {
    ...
```

7. Add getters and setters for the columns that we have created in Parse using the following code:

```
public void setCustomer (String value) {
    put("customer", value);
}
public String getCustomer (){
    return getString("customer");
```

```
    }
    public void setAddress (String value) {
        put("address", value);
    }
    public String getAddress (){
        return getString("address");
    }
```

8. Now, tell Parse about this new class. In the `CloudOrderApplication` class, add this line right before the `Parse.Initialize` line:

```
ParseObject.registerSubclass(CloudOrder.class);
```

9. To get the cloud orders in our app, we need to define a query indicating what exactly it is that we are looking for. In its most basic form, query looks like the following snippet. Add it to the `onCreate` method of `MainActivity`:

```
ParseQuery<ParseObject> query = ParseQuery.getQuery("CloudOrder");
```

10. We are going to tell Parse that we want to perform this query asynchronously by using the `findInBackground` method. Add the following lines to do so:

```
query.findInBackground(new FindCallback<ParseObject>() {
    public void done(List<ParseObject> items, ParseException e) {
        if (e==null){
            Log.i("TEST", String.format("%d objects found", items.
size()));
        }
    }
});
```

11. Run the app and check **LogCat** (use the shortcut *Cmd + 6* to make it appear). It displays the number of objects that have been found. This should return the numbers of rows that you have created for **CargoOrder** at `www.parse.com`.

12. Great! Now, if only we had an adapter to make these items available in the list view. Create a new class and name it `CloudOrderAdapter`. Make it an array adapter descendant with the `CloudOrder` type:

```
public class CloudOrderAdapter extends ArrayAdapter<CloudOrder> {
...
```

13. Implement the constructor, create a view holder, and add the implementation for all the methods that need to be overridden. Finally, your adapter will look like this:

```
public class CloudOrderAdapter extends ArrayAdapter<CloudOrder> {
    private Context mContext;
    private int mAdapterResourceId;
    public ArrayList<CloudOrder> mItems = null;
    static class ViewHolder{
```

```
            TextView customer;
            TextView address;
        }
        @Override
        public int getCount(){
            super.getCount();
            int count = mItems !=null ? mItems.size()  :  0;
            return count;
        }
        public CloudOrderAdapter (Context context, int
adapterResourceId, ArrayList<CloudOrder>items) {
            super(context, adapterResourceId, items);
            this.mItems = items;
            this.mContext = context;
            this.mAdapterResourceId = adapterResourceId;
        }
        @Override
        public View getView(int position, View convertView, ViewGroup
parent) {
            View v = null;
            v = convertView;
            if (v == null){
                LayoutInflater vi = (LayoutInflater)this.getContext().
    getSystemService(Context.LAYOUT_INFLATER_SERVICE);
                v = vi.inflate(mAdapterResourceId, null);
                ViewHolder holder = new ViewHolder();
                holder.customer = (TextView) v.findViewById(R.
id.adapter_main_customer);
                holder.address = (TextView)v.findViewById(R.
id.adapter_main_address);
                v.setTag(holder);
            }
            final CloudOrder item = mItems.get(position);
            if(item != null){
                final ViewHolder holder = (ViewHolder)v.getTag();
                holder.customer.setText(item.getCustomer());
                holder.address.setText(item.getAddress());
            }
            return v;
        }
    }
```

14. Go back to the `MainActivity` class and modify the code of the query call back so that we can feed our newly created adapter with the results over there, like this:

```
ParseQuery<ParseObject> query = ParseQuery.getQuery("CloudOrder");

query.findInBackground(new FindCallback<ParseObject>(){
    public void done(List<ParseObject> items, ParseException e) {
        Object result = items;
        if (e == null){
            ArrayList<CloudOrder> orders = (ArrayList<CloudOrder>)
result;
            Log.i("TEST", String.format("%d objects found",
orders.size()));
            CloudOrderAdapter adapter = new CloudOrderAdapter
(getApplicationContext(), R.layout.adapter_main, orders);
            ListView listView = (ListView)findViewById(R.id.main_
list_orders);
            listView.setAdapter(adapter);;
        }
    }
});
```

15. To display the orders in our app, we have to create a layout for it. Expand the `layout` folder and double-click on the `activity_main.xml` file to open it. By default, a preview of the layout is shown. Change the perspective to text by clicking on the **Text** tab at the bottom of Android Studio, which makes the layout display as XML.

16. Remove the **TextView** widget that displays `Hello world` and add a list view:

```
<ListView
    android:id="@+id/main_list_orders"
    android:layout_width="wrap_content"
    android:layout_height="match_parent"/>
```

17. Select the `layout` folder again and right-click on it. From the menu, choose **New**, and from the submenu, choose **Layout resource**. Choose `adapter_main` for the File name and click on the **OK** button. A new layout file will be created. Change the perspective from design to text.

18. Add two text views to the layout so that we can display both the customer name and the address and add some formatting, like this:

```
<?xml version="1.0" encoding="utf-8"?>
<LinearLayout xmlns:android="http://schemas.android.com/apk/res/
android"
    android:orientation="vertical" android:layout_width="match_
parent"
    android:padding="8dp" android:layout_height="match_parent">
    <TextView
        android:text="(Customer)"
```

```
        android:textStyle="bold"
        android:textSize="20sp"
        android:textColor="@android:color/black"
        android:id="@+id/adapter_main_customer"
        android:layout_width="match_parent"
        android:layout_height="wrap_content" />
    <TextView
        android:text="(Address)"
        android:textSize="16sp"
        android:textColor="@android:color/darker_gray"
        android:id="@+id/adapter_main_address"
        android:layout_width="match_parent"
        android:layout_height="wrap_content" />
</LinearLayout>
```

19. You are done. Run your app. If everything goes well, you will see an output like the one shown in the following screenshot, and this is what your list view may look like after having the orders consumed from `www.parse.com`:

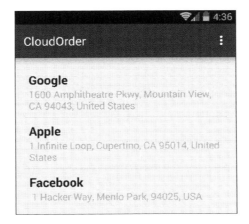

20. If you run into a `class exception error`, have a look again at step 8. Did you register your `ParseOrder` subclass? In case you are running into any other errors, repeat each step carefully to check whether there are any missing parts or mismatches.

There's more...

This recipe is nothing but a brief introduction to Parse. At `www.parse.com`, you will find much more information about how to retrieve data from a cloud, including using **where** and **order by** statements in your queries. It also provides you with information that is needed to create relational or compound queries.

Submitting data to the cloud

Now that we have completed the previous recipes and the driver that will be using our `CloudOrder` app knows where to go to for a particular order, it would be great if, once the goods are delivered, he (or she) will be able to select that order and have it signed for delivery by the customer on the device.

In this last recipe, we will implement code to make the customer draws his or her signature on the device. The signature will be sent to Parse as an image and the `CloudOrder` record will be updated.

Getting ready

To go through this recipe, you will need to have the previous recipes up and running.

How to do it...

1. Create a new class and name it `SignatureActivity`.

2. Create a new layout and name it `activity_signature.xml`.

3. Switch the layout to **Text**. Add the **TextView** and the **Button** widget to the layout. Make sure that the layout looks like this:

    ```xml
    <?xml version="1.0" encoding="utf-8"?>
    <LinearLayout xmlns:android="http://schemas.android.com/apk/res/
    android"
        android:orientation="vertical" android:layout_width="match_
    parent"
        android:padding="8dp" android:layout_height="match_parent">
        <TextView
            android:id="@+id/signature_text"
            android:text=" Please sign here:"
            android:textSize="24sp"
            android:textColor="@android:color/black"
            android:layout_width="match_parent"
            android:layout_height="wrap_content" />
        <Button
            android:id="@+id/signature_button"
            android:text="Send signature"
            android:layout_width="match_parent"
            android:layout_height="wrap_content" />
    </LinearLayout>
    ```

4. To allow the customer to draw his signature, we need to create a custom widget.

5. Right under the `com.packt.cloudorder` package, create a new package and name it `widget`.

6. Within this new package, create a new class and name it `SignatureView`.

7. Make the `SignatureView` class descend from the `View` class and override the `onDraw` method to draw a path wherever we put our finger or stylus on the screen. Override the `onTouch` method to create the path. snippet for creating the path will look like this:

```
package com.packt.cloudorder.widget;
import android.content.Context;
import android.graphics.Bitmap;
import android.graphics.Canvas;
import android.graphics.Color;
import android.graphics.Paint;
import android.graphics.Path;
import android.graphics.drawable.Drawable;
import android.util.AttributeSet;
import android.view.MotionEvent;
import android.view.View;
public class SignatureView extends View {
    private Paint paint = new Paint();
    private Path path = new Path();
    public SignatureView(Context context, AttributeSet attrs) {
        super(context, attrs);
        paint.setAntiAlias(true);
        paint.setStrokeWidth(3f);
        paint.setColor(Color.BLACK);
        paint.setStyle(Paint.Style.STROKE);
        paint.setStrokeJoin(Paint.Join.ROUND);
    }
    @Override
    protected void onDraw(Canvas canvas) {
        canvas.drawPath(path, paint);
    }
    @Override
    public boolean onTouchEvent(MotionEvent event) {
        float eventX = event.getX();
        float eventY = event.getY();
        switch (event.getAction()) {
            case MotionEvent.ACTION_DOWN:
                path.moveTo(eventX, eventY);
                return true;
            case MotionEvent.ACTION_MOVE:
                path.lineTo(eventX, eventY);
```

```
                break;
            case MotionEvent.ACTION_UP:
                break;
            default:
                return false;
        }
        invalidate();
        return true;
    }
```

8. Add the `getSignatureBitmap` method to the `SignatureView` class so that we can get the signature as a bitmap from the `Signature` view widget:

```
public Bitmap getSignatureBitmap() {
        Bitmap result = Bitmap.createBitmap(getWidth(),
    getHeight(), Bitmap.Config.ARGB_8888);
        Canvas canvas = new Canvas(result);
        Drawable bgDrawable =getBackground();
        if (bgDrawable!=null) {
            bgDrawable.draw(canvas);
        }else {
            canvas.drawColor(Color.WHITE);
            draw(canvas);
        }
        return result;
    }
}
```

9. Go back to the `signature_activity` layout and add the signature view between the text view and the button:

```
<com.packt.cloudorder.widget.SignatureView
    android:id="@+id/signature_view"
    android:layout_width="match_parent"
    android:layout_height="200dp"
    android:layout_marginLeft="3dp"
    android:layout_marginTop="3dp"
    android:layout_marginRight="0dp"
    android:layout_marginBottom="18dp"/>
```

10. Build the project. It should make any rendering issues disappear.

11. Implement the `SignatureActivity` class. First, make it an `Activity` descendant and override the `onCreate` method. Set the content view to the layout we have just created and add an `onClick` implementation for the button in the layout, like this:

```
public class SignatureActivity  extends Activity {
    @Override
    protected void onCreate(Bundle savedInstanceState) {
```

```
        super.onCreate(savedInstanceState);
        setContentView(R.layout.activity_signature);
        findViewById(R.id.signature_button).setOnClickListener(new
    View.OnClickListener(){
            @Override
            public void onClick(View v) {
            }
        });
    }
}
```

12. Add the activity to the manifest file after the `MainActivity` declaration as follows:

```
<activity android:name=".SignatureActivity"/>
```

13. If the driver selects any of the orders, we need to display the signature activity that in turn needs to know which order has been selected. Go to the `MainActivity` class and append `OnItemClickListener` on the list view at the end of the `OnCreate` method, just after the `Query.findInBackground` call:

```
((ListView)findViewById(R.id.main_list_orders)).
setOnItemClickListener(new AdapterView.OnItemClickListener() {
    @Override
    public void onItemClick(AdapterView<?> parent, View view, int
position, long id) {
    }
});
```

14. In the `onItemClick` event, let's figure out which order has been selected using the following code snippet:

```
ListView listView = (ListView)findViewById(R.id.main_list_orders);
CloudOrder order = (CloudOrder)listView.getAdapter().
getItem(position);
gotoSignatureActivity(order);
```

15. In the `gotoSignatureActivity` method, we want to start the `Signature` activity, using an intent, and pass the selected order from `MainActivity` to `SignatureActivity`, using a bundle as shown:

```
private void gotoSignatureActivity(CloudOrder order){
    Intent intent = new Intent(this, SignatureActivity.class);
    Bundle extras = new Bundle();
    extras.putString("orderId", order.getObjectId());
    intent.putExtras(extras);
    this.startActivity(intent);
}
```

16. In the `SignatureActivity` class, add the following to the `OnClick` implementation of the button:

```
sendSignature();
```

17. For the `sendSignature` method implementation, we will create a new `ParseFile` object and feed it with the bitmap data that comes from the signature view. We will send the file to Parse using the `saveInBackground` method:

```
private void sendSignature() {
    final Activity activity = this;
    SignatureView signatureView = (SignatureView)findViewById(R.
id.signature_view);
    ByteArrayOutputStream stream = new ByteArrayOutputStream();
    signatureView.getSignatureBitmap().compress(Bitmap.
CompressFormat.PNG, 100, stream);
    byte[] data = stream.toByteArray();
    final ParseFile file = new ParseFile("signature.jpg", data);
    file.saveInBackground(new SaveCallback() {
        @Override
        public void done(com.parse.ParseException e) {
        }
    });
}
```

18. Once the saving is done, we want to update the order with information about the file we have created and the status, for example `10`, which could indicate that the order has been finished or something like that. Its actually value does not really matter here.

19. If no error occurred during saving, we use the `createWithoutData` method of the `ParseObject` class so that we could pass the right object ID and the fields that we want to update. We will save these changes as well so that the record at Parse will be updated. (For the sake of simplicity, we use this approach; although, we could accomplish the same thing using the `CloudOrder` object) The implementation of the done call back looks like this:

```
if (e == null) {
 Bundle extras = getIntent().getExtras();
ParseObject order = ParseObject.createWithoutData("CloudOrder",
    extras.getString("orderId"));
                order.put("signature", file);
                order.put("status", 10);

                order.saveInBackground(new SaveCallback() {
                    @Override
                    public void done(ParseException e) {
                        if (e==null){
```

```
                                Toast.makeText(activity, "Signature
has been sent!", Toast.LENGTH_SHORT).show();
                                }
                        }
                });
```

20. Run the app, select an order, sign it, and click on the **SEND SIGNATURE** button. If everything goes well, a toast will be shown, indicating that the signature has been sent.

    This is what your signature looks like after signing by a customer:

21. Check it out for yourself at www.parse.com. Refresh the view for **Cloud order**. Notice that for the order that you have selected in the app, the signature.jpg file appears in the signature column. Double-click on it to see its contents. This is what your data rows may look like at www.parse.com after submitting a signature image to it:

Actually, you should be using string resources instead of hardcoded values. By reusing string resources (or constant values) not only for the class and field names but also for other texts, you will reduce the number of errors caused by typos. This will improve the quality of your app. It also will make it much easier to localize your app later. (In the last three chapters, we will focus more on these kind of things but here is some good practice to start with right away.) The following steps gives usage of string resources:

1. Check out the `strings.xml` file. It resides in the `res/values` folder. Imagine we would have included the text for the toast being displayed in step 19. Your `strings.xml` file could look like this:

```xml
<?xml version="1.0" encoding="utf-8"?>
<resources>
    …
        <string name="app_name">Cloud order</string>
        <string name="parse_class_cargo_order">CargoOrder</string>
        <string name="signature_send">Your signature has been sent.</string>
    . . .
```

2. In your code, you could refer to a string resource using the `getString` method. You could replace the hardcoded string for the toast being displayed in step 19 for example with a string reference, like this:

```java
Toast.makeText(activity, getString(R.string.signature_send),
Toast.LENGTH_SHORT).show();
```

3. In your layout file, you could also refer to this string resource, for example, in a text view:

```xml
<TextView
    android:text="@string/signature_send"
    android:layout_width="wrap_content"
    android:layout_height="match_parent" />
```

We will describe how to use strings, colors, dimensions, and other type of resources in depth later, but you can already get a bit familiar with the concepts by replacing all hardcoded strings in this recipe with string resource references or where applicable, use constant values for them.

With the implementation of this recipe, we have completed our `CloudOrder` app. Feel free to further customize it and make enhancements wherever you want to.

How it works...

The custom widget draws a path on the view, for which a bitmap will be created. Using a `ParseFile` object, the bitmap data will be send to Parse (which in turn will store the file in Amazon and keep a reference to the file).

If this succeeds, we will update the **CloudOrder** row to which the signature applies by denoting to which file the image in the **signature** column refers to.

There's more...

Have a closer look at the documentation at `www.parse.com`. There are a couple of interesting features available including the `saveEventually` method and the cloud code options.

The `saveEventually` method will store the update locally if there is no Internet connection available, which is a common scenario for mobile apps. Once the Internet connection has been restored, this method will take of, sending the data that has been queued to be sent to the cloud. This option will save you much troubles and time.

Also check out the other features such as cloud code and the various third-party integrations that are available, such as Twilio, if you want to send text or voice messages (which could be handy for confirmation purposes in on-boarding processes) and SendGrid, which is a tool for e-mail delivery.

Following the recipes in this chapter, we have implemented some very interesting functionalities with little effort, which is really great! The app however is not very eye-catching yet. By applying the concepts of Material design, which will be explained in the next chapter, we can make the app look great and more intuitive to use.

See also

> ▸ For more information, refer to *Chapter 3, Material Design*.

3
Material Design

This chapter will teach you what material design is about, why it is such a great improvement, and why you should use it for your apps.

In this chapter, you will learn about:

- ▸ Recycler views and card views
- ▸ Ripples and elevations
- ▸ Great transitions

Introduction

With the introduction of material design, the looks of Android apps will finally mature. They can compete very well with iOS designs. Android material apps have a flat design, but come with some interesting differences such as elevations. Consider the following figure for example:

Think of it as multiple slides of paper. It is based on, well, materials. Each slide of paper has a particular elevation. So, the environment is in fact a 3D world with effects such as light and shadow. Any motion should have real-world behaviour as if the moved elements are real physical objects. Animation is another important element of material design.

First have a look at `https://www.google.co.in/design/spec/material-design/introduction.html` to see what material design is all about. Sure, many things are interesting for designers in particular, and you probably are interested only in the implementation of all this beautiful stuff; however, this link provides you with a little bit more context about what material design is about.

For a long time, most Android apps suffered from bad design or, in the early days no design at all. Or, they looked pretty similar to those made for iPhone, including all the elements that are typical for iOS.

Have a look at the next app screenshot:

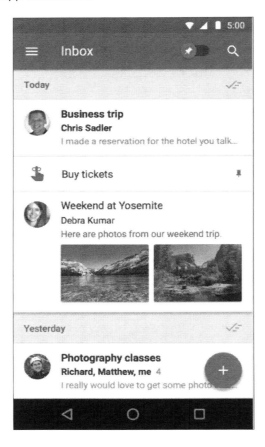

Using Material design, this is what most of Google apps look like nowadays.

Many Google's apps for Android use material design now. They all follow the same guidelines for interaction and design. The interface is minimalistic, as one would expect from Google. Also, the interface has become more uniform, making it easier to understand and use.

Earlier, responsiveness was something you had to take care of yourself. Material design comes with ripples and other effects, doing the same thing, which is providing feedback on user input, but it is much easier to implement and is much more elegant.

As for the components, material design dictates for example how buttons in a particular situation should look. Think of floating buttons used for actions, or flat buttons used in dialog boxes. It also replaces the **ListView** with **RecyclerView**, which provide more flexibility to show lists. **CardViews** are common elements and you can see them being used in the Google apps quite often. Various animations provide more natural transitions, such as those for navigational or scrolling purposes.

Material design is not just for the latest and greatest. While it comes with Android Lollipop (5.0) and higher versions, most material design features can be used in Android version 2.1 and up via the `v7 support` libraries, which allow us to apply a material design and still support virtually almost all Android devices.

Altogether, material design provides quite a lot to the beautification of your app. People want to be beautiful too. Health apps are booming because of this. Finding out what is healthy to eat, suggesting to drink more water, and advising on running or fitness exercises are common objectives that come with these type of apps. To demonstrate the beauty of Material design, we will be creating an app that will help people become healthier.

So, what about a `drink water and take a selfie` app? People need to drink water more often and if they do, they could see the effect of it. Beautiful people deserve a beautiful app. This makes sense, does it not?

Reycler views and card views

The recycler view replaces the good old list view. It provides more flexibility in how the elements of a list are shown, for example, as a grid and as horizontal or vertical items. Instead of rows, we can now choose to display cards wherever it is suitable.

In our app, each card should display some text about the entry and a thumbnail of the picture that we took. This is what this recipe will be all about.

Getting ready

To go through this recipe, you need to have Android up and running. Also make sure that you have installed the latest SDK. (You can check whether you have the latest SDK by opening the SDK manager). To do so, open the **Tools** menu, choose **Android**, and next, choose the **SDK Manager** option.

How to do it...

Let's investigate, using the following steps, how to use recycler views and cards:

1. Start Android Studio and start a new project. Name your application `WaterApp` and enter `packtpub.com` in the **Company Domain** field. Then, click on the **Next** button.

2. Choose **Blank Activity** in the next dialog box and click on the **Next** button.

3. In the following dialog box, click on the **Finish** button.

4. Open the `build.gradle` file within your `app` folder and add the dependency for the recycler view to the `dependencies` section as shown in the following code:

```
dependencies {
    compile fileTree(dir: 'libs', include: ['*.jar'])
    compile 'com.android.support:appcompat-v7:22.1.1'
    compile 'com.android.support:recyclerview-v7:+'
}
```

5. Change `minSdkVersion` to at least `21` in the `build.gradle` file.

 This does not really have to be the minimal required version, but since the support libraries for backward compatibility purposes do not contain all of the Material design features, I have chosen to pick API level 21 here, just to be on the safe side.

6. Synchronize your project by clicking on the **Sync now** label on the yellow bar that appears after we edit the `build.gradle` file, or in case it does not, click on the **Sync Project with Gradle files** button on the toolbar.

7. Open the `activity_main.xml` layout file, remove the `Hello World TextView`, and add a `RecyclerView` tag to the layout, like this:

```
<android.support.v7.widget.RecyclerView
    android:id="@+id/main_recycler_view"
    android:scrollbars="vertical"
    android:layout_width="match_parent"
    android:layout_height="match_parent"/>
```

8. In your `MainActivity` class, add the following to the `onCreate` method just after `setContentView`:

```
RecyclerView recyclerView = (RecyclerView)
  findViewById(R.id.main_recycler_view);
```

9. The `RecyclerView` class is not a known class yet. Use the *Alt + Enter* shortcut to add the right import statement or add the following line yourself:

```
import android.support.v7.widget.RecyclerView;
```

10. We are going to use a linear layout manager for this recipe. Add the following lines after the line we have added in step 9:

```
LinearLayoutManager layoutManager = new LinearLayoutManager(this);
recyclerView.setLayoutManager(layoutManager);
```

11. Create a new package and name it `models`, and within this package, create a new `Drink` class as follows:

```
package com.packt.waterapp.models;
import java.util.Date;
public class Drink {
    public Date dateAndTime;
    public String comments;
    public String imageUri;
}
```

Here, the `Date` class refers to the `java.util.Date` package (this is specified since there is also a SQL-related class with the same class name).

12. Let's create a layout to display the items. Right-click on the `layout` package in the project tree and create a new resource file. To do so, choose **New** and **New Layout Resource File** from the menu. Name it `adapter_main.xml` and hit the **OK** button.

13. Switch the layout to the **Text** modus, change the orientation of `LinearLayout` from `vertical` to `horizontal`, add some padding to it and add an image view to it, as shown in the following snippet. We will also add a default image so that we have something to look at:

```
<?xml version="1.0" encoding="utf-8"?>
<LinearLayout
xmlns:android="http://schemas.android.com/apk/res/android"
android:orientation="horizontal" android:layout_width="match_
parent"
android:padding="8dp" android:layout_height="match_parent">
<ImageView android:id="@+id/main_image_view"
android:src="@android:drawable/ic_menu_camera"
android:scaleType="center"
android:layout_width="90dp"
android:layout_height="90dp" />
</LinearLayout>
```

14. Next to the image, we want to display a date and time and the comments using two `TextView` widgets wrapped in another `LinearLayout` widget. Add these after the `ImageView` tag:

```
<LinearLayout
    android:orientation="vertical"
    android:layout_width="match_parent"
    android:layout_height="wrap_content">
```

```xml
    <TextView
        android:id="@+id/main_date_time_textview"
        android:layout_marginTop="8dp"
        android:textSize="12sp"
        android:textColor="@color/material_blue_grey_800"
        android:layout_width="match_parent"
        android:layout_height="wrap_content" />
    <TextView
        android:id="@+id/main_comment_textview"
        android:layout_marginTop="16dp"
        android:maxLines="3"
        android:textSize="16sp"
        android:textColor="@color/material_deep_teal_500"
        android:layout_width="match_parent"
        android:layout_height="wrap_content" />
</LinearLayout>
```

15. Create another package and name it `adapters`. Within that package, create the `MainAdapter` class that will be using a `ViewHolder` class, helping us to display the data exactly where we want it to appear. We also include all methods that need to be overridden such as the `onBindViewHolder` method and the `getItemCount` method:

```java
public class MainAdapter extends RecyclerView.Adapter<MainAdapter.
ViewHolder> {
    private ArrayList<Drink> mDrinks;
    private Context mContext;
    public static class ViewHolder extends
      RecyclerView.ViewHolder {
      public TextView mCommentTextView;
      public TextView mDateTimeTextView;
      public ImageView mImageView;
      public ViewHolder(View v) {
          super(v);
      }
    }
    public MainAdapter(Context context,
      ArrayList<Drink> drinks) {
      mDrinks = drinks;
      mContext = context;
    }
    @Override
    public MainAdapter.ViewHolder
     onCreateViewHolder(ViewGroup parent,  int viewType) {
        View v = LayoutInflater.from(
         parent.getContext()).inflate(
           R.layout.adapter_main, parent, false);
        ViewHolder viewHolder = new ViewHolder(v);
        viewHolder.mDateTimeTextView =
```

```
      (TextView)v.findViewById(
        R.id.main_date_time_textview);
      viewHolder.mCommentTextView =
        (TextView)v.findViewById(
        R.id.main_comment_textview);
      viewHolder.mImageView =
        (ImageView)v.findViewById(
        R.id.main_image_view);
      return viewHolder;
    }
    @Override
    public int getItemCount() {
      return mDrinks.size();
    }
  }
}
```

16. We have more things to do. Add the onBindViewHolder method and add the implementation to actually bind the data to the right widgets:

```
@Override
public void onBindViewHolder(ViewHolder holder,
    int position) {
    Drink currentDrink = mDrinks.get(position);
    holder.mCommentTextView.setText(
      currentDrink.comments);
    holder.mDateTimeTextView.setText(
      currentDrink.dateAndTime.toString());
    if (currentDrink.imageUri != null){
        holder.mImageView.setImageURI(
          Uri.parse(currentDrink.imageUri));
    }
}
```

17. In the MainActivity file, we need to have an instance of the adapter and some data to display. Add a private adapter and a private array list containing the Drink items:

```
private MainAdapter mAdapter;
private ArrayList<Drink> mDrinks;
```

18. At the end of the onCreate method, tell recyclerView which adapter to use and tell the adapter which dataset to use:

```
mAdapter = new MainAdapter(this, mDrinks);
recyclerView.setAdapter(mAdapter);
```

19. In the `MainActivity` file, we want to add some dummy data so that we have some idea about what things are going to look like. Add the following to the `onCreate` method just before the part where we create the `MainAdapter` class:

```
mDrinks = new ArrayList<Drink>();
Drink firstDrink = new Drink();
firstDrink.comments = "I like water with bubbles most of the
time...";
firstDrink.dateAndTime = new Date();
mDrinks.add(firstDrink);
Drink secondDrink = new Drink();
secondDrink.comments = "I also like water without bubbles. It
depends on my mood I guess ;-)";
secondDrink.dateAndTime = new Date();
mDrinks.add(secondDrink);
```

Import the required packages using the *Alt + enter* shortcut.

Run your app to verify that everything has gone well so far. Your app will display two entries containing the sample data that we have created in the previous step.

Using card views

The app looks okay but I would not want to call it beautiful yet. Let's see if we can improve this a little. The following steps will help us to create the app using card views:

1. Open the `build.gradle` file in the `app` folder and add a `CardView` dependency, just after the one for the recycler view:

```
compile 'com.android.support:cardview-v7:+'
```

And synchronize your project again.

 By the way, if this app was for real, then avoid unpleasant surprises by specifying an exact version instead of using the + sign in the version number for any dependency your app may have. Currently, this is `21.0.0` for this particular dependency, but By the time you read this, a new version might be available.

2. If an error appears indicating Gradle failed to resolve the card view dependency, then click on the **Install Repository and sync project** link, accept the license, and click on the **Next** button. Wait a while until the download is complete and the installation has finished. Once this is done, click on the **Finish** button. Sync your project again.

3. Create a new layout and name it `adapter_main_card_view.xml`. Add some padding to the `LinearLayout` tag and within the `linear layout` tag, add a `CardView`:

```
<?xml version="1.0" encoding="utf-8"?> <LinearLayout
xmlns:android="http://schemas.android.com/apk/res/android"
    android:orientation="vertical"
```

```
        android:layout_width="match_parent"
        android:padding="4dp"
        android:layout_height="match_parent">
        <android.support.v7.widget.CardView
            xmlns:card_view=
            "http://schemas.android.com/apk/res-auto"
             android:id="@+id/card_view"
            android:layout_gravity="center"
            android:layout_width="match_parent"
            android:layout_height="wrap_content"
             card_view:cardCornerRadius="4dp">
        </android.support.v7.widget.CardView>
    </LinearLayout>
```

4. From the previous layout, the `adapter_main.xml` file, copy `ImageView` and the two `TextView` widgets (but not `LinearLayout` that contains the two `TextView` widgets) and paste them within `CardView` that you have added to the `adapter_main_card_view.xml` file.

5. Because `CardView` behaves as if it is `FrameLayout`, you need to set the margins for the text labels. Add a left margin to both text views. Also modify the top margin for the `TextView` comment:

```
<TextView
    android:id="@+id/main_date_time_textview"
    android:layout_marginTop="8dp"
    android:layout_marginLeft="100dp"
    android:textSize="12sp"
    android:textColor="@color/material_blue_grey_800"
    android:layout_width="match_parent"
    android:layout_height="wrap_content" />
<TextView
    android:id="@+id/main_comment_textview"
    android:layout_marginTop="32dp"
    android:layout_marginLeft="100dp"
    android:maxLines="3"
    android:textSize="16sp"
    android:textColor="@color/material_deep_teal_500"
    android:layout_width="match_parent"
    android:layout_height="wrap_content" />
```

6. Now you tell the `MainAdapter` class to use this layout by changing the layout ID in the `onCreateViewHolder` method:

```
View v = LayoutInflater.from(parent.getContext()). inflate(R.
layout.adapter_main_card_view, parent, false);
```

Run the app again and we will see what it will look like this time:

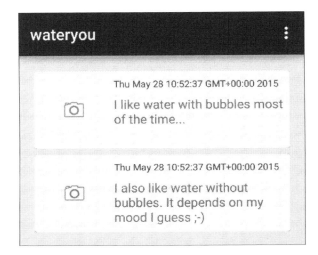

7. In the next recipe, we will add an elevated floating button and we will create a new activity that allows the users of our app to add drinks, comments, and a selfie.

There's more...

There is a lot of documentation about material design. Browse through the various examples that are available on various websites, such as `https://www.materialup.com`, `http://materialdesignblog.com` or `http://material-design.tumblr.com`.

Or, download some of the material designed apps that are available in the Play Store, such as the Inbox, Google+, Wunderlist, Evernote, LocalCast, and SoundCast apps.

Ripples and elevations

While elevations and ripples are not exactly to be considered to make people more beautiful, applying these and other material design principles to our app will certainly contribute to the beautification of it.

In the previous recipe, we created a list to show all logged drinks. In this recipe we will add an elevated button to add new entries. Also, we will create a new activity.

For each entry, the user can describe some thoughts on what he drank. Of course, the user has to be able to take a selfie each time so that later he can check whether drinking all that water or green tea (or beer for that matter, if the user of our app does have a slightly different objective than that this app has been intended for) indeed did have a positive effect on his health and his (or her) looks.

Getting ready

For this recipe, it would be great if you have the previous recipe completed as this will build upon our previous achievements.

How to do it...

Let's add a floating button and create a new activity to edit new entries:

1. Add a new drawable resource file to the `res/drawable` folder, name it `button_round_teal_bg.xml`, and hit the **OK** button.

2. Using XML, we will create a round oval shape for the button. Remove the selector tags first (if any). Wrap it up in a `ripple` tag. A `ripple` provides visible feedback in case the button is being pressed; I have chosen a material design variant of teal as the color but you can of course pick any color that you like. For inspiration, you could check out `http://www.google.com/design/spec/style/ color.html`. The content for the file looks like as shown in the following example:

```xml
<ripple xmlns:android="http://schemas.android.com/apk/res/android"
    android:color="#009789">
    <item>
        <shape android:shape="oval">
            <solid android:color="?android:colorAccent"/>
        </shape>
    </item>
</ripple>
```

 In case you run into any error, check `minSdkVersion` in the `build.gradle` file. Refer to step 5 of the first recipe for further information.

3. Add a button to the `activity_main.xml` layout file just after the recycler view:

```xml
<ImageButton
    android:id="@+id/main_button_add"
    android:elevation="1dp"
    android:layout_width="48dp"
    android:layout_height="48dp"
    android:layout_alignParentBottom="true"
    android:layout_alignParentRight="true"
    android:layout_margin="16dp"
    android:tint="@android:color/white"
    android:background="@drawable/button_round_teal_bg"
    android:src="@android:drawable/ic_input_add"/>
```

Colors should be defined in a separate color resource file. Also, elevations and margins should be placed in a dimension resource file. Since this is out of scope for this recipe, I suggest you do this later.

4. Next we want to have some shadows, and also we want to change the elevation if the button is being pushed or released. Create a new directory in the `res` folder and name it `anim`. Within this folder, create a new animation resource file. Name the file `button_elevation.xml` and hit the **OK** button:

```
<selector xmlns:android="http://schemas.android.com/apk/res/
android">
    <item android:state_pressed="true">
        <objectAnimator
            android:propertyName="translationZ"android:duration="@
android:integer/config_shortAnimTime"
            android:valueFrom="1dp"
            android:valueTo="4dp"
            android:valueType="floatType"/>
    </item>
    <item>
        <objectAnimator
            android:propertyName="translationZ"
 android:duration="@android:integer/config_shortAnimTime"
            android:valueFrom="4dp"
            android:valueTo="1dp"
            android:valueType="floatType"/>
    </item>
</selector>
```

5. Inform the image button about this new resource file. In your `activity_main.xml` layout, add the following line to your image button:

```
android:stateListAnimator="@anim/button_elevation"
```

6. At the end of the onCreate method in the MainActivity class add an `OnClickListener` to the button that we just created and call the `showEntry` method, which we will be creating in a minute or two:

```
findViewById(R.id.main_button_add).setOnClickListener(new
 View.OnClickListener() {
    @Override
    public void onClick(View v) {
        showEntry();}
});
```

7. Create a new layout resource file, name it `activity_entry.xml`, and use `FrameLayout` as the root element. Then hit the **OK** button.

8. Add an `EditText` widget for comments, a button to take pictures and another button to save the entry. Then wrap these elements in a `CardView` widget. Add an `ImageView` widget after the `CardView` widget, like this:

```xml
<?xml version="1.0" encoding="utf-8"?>
<FrameLayout xmlns:android=
 "http://schemas.android.com/apk/res/android"
    android:padding="8dp" android:layout_width="match_parent"
    android:layout_height="match_parent">
    <android.support.v7.widget.CardView xmlns:card_view="http://
schemas.android.com/apk/res-auto"
        android:id="@+id/card_view"
        android:layout_width="match_parent"
        android:layout_height="200dp"
        card_view:cardCornerRadius="4dp">
    <EditText
        android:id="@+id/entry_edit_text_comment"
        android:lines="6"
        android:layout_width="match_parent"
        android:layout_height="wrap_content"
        android:layout_marginRight="60dp"/>
    <ImageButton
        android:id="@+id/entry_image_button_camera"
        android:src="@android:drawable/ic_menu_camera"
        android:layout_gravity="right"
        android:layout_width="wrap_content"
        android:layout_height="wrap_content" />
    <Button
        android:id="@+id/entry_button_add"
        android:layout_gravity="bottom"
        android:text="Add entry"
        android:layout_width="match_parent"
        android:layout_height="wrap_content" />
    </android.support.v7.widget.CardView>
    <ImageView
        android:id="@+id/entry_image_view_preview"
        android:scaleType="fitCenter"
        android:layout_marginTop="210dp"
        android:layout_width="match_parent"
        android:layout_height="match_parent" />
</FrameLayout>
```

9. Create a new class, name it `EntryActivity`, and click on the **OK** button.

10. Make your class descend from `Activity`, override the `onCreate` method, and set the content view to the layout that you just created:

```
public class EntryActivity extends Activity {
    @Override
    protected void onCreate(Bundle savedInstanceState) {
        super.onCreate(savedInstanceState);
        setContentView(R.layout.activity_entry);
    }
}
```

11. Do not forget to add your new activity in the `AndroidManifest.xml` file:

```
<activity android:name=".EntryActivity"/>
```

12. In the `MainActivity` class, add the `showEntry` method and the implementation that is needed to display the new activity. We will be using the `startActivityForResult` method here because this will allow the `EntryActivity` to return data later:

```
private int REQUEST_NEW_ENTRY = 1;
private void showEntry(){
    Intent intent = new Intent(this, EntryActivity.class);
    startActivityForResult(intent, REQUEST_NEW_ENTRY);
}
```

Now if you run the app and push the button, you will notice the visual feedback. To see the effect properly, you may want to use a stylus or enlarge the size of the button. If you release the button, you will see the entry layout. In the layout, if you push (and hold) the **Add entry** button (or the camera button), you will notice the ripple effect. We did not have to do anything special for that. With the introduction of Lollipop (and previous description), this is the default behavior for buttons. However, these buttons do look a bit boring and as you have seen with the floating button, there are plenty of customization options available. Let's follow the next steps:

1. In the `EntryActivity` class, set the `OnClickListener` for the camera button and do the same thing for the `add` button:

```
findViewById(R.id.entry_image_button_camera).setOnClickListener(
  new View.OnClickListener() {
    @Override
    public void onClick(View v) {
        takePicture();
    }
});
findViewById(R.id.entry_button_add).setOnClickListener(new
  View.OnClickListener() {
    @Override
    public void onClick(View v) {
    }
});
```

2. Add a private member that will contain the URI for the photo that we are going to take:

```
private Uri mUri;
```

3. Create a `takePicture` method and add the implementation for it. We will create a file with a unique image name up front by using a time stamp and we will tell the image capture intent to use `Uri` for that file:

```
private int REQUEST_IMAGE_CAPTURE = 1;
private void takePicture(){
    File  filePhoto = new
    File(Environment.getExternalStorageDirectory(),
      String.valueOf(new Date().getTime())+"selfie.jpg");
    mUri = Uri.fromFile(filePhoto);
    Intent intent = new
     Intent("android.media.action.IMAGE_CAPTURE");
    intent.putExtra(MediaStore.EXTRA_OUTPUT, mUri);
    startActivityForResult(intent, REQUEST_IMAGE_CAPTURE);
}
```

4. Override the `onActivityResult` method that will be triggered once a photo has been taken. If everything goes well, we need to create a bitmap of the file we just created by taking the picture and show a preview of it:

```
@Override
protected void onActivityResult(int requestCode, int resultCode,
  Intent data) {
    super.onActivityResult(requestCode, resultCode, data);
    if (requestCode == REQUEST_IMAGE_CAPTURE &&
        resultCode == RESULT_OK){
        Bitmap bitmap = getBitmapFromUri();
        ImageView preview = (ImageView)
          findViewById(R.id.entry_image_view_preview);
        preview.setImageBitmap(bitmap);
    }
}
```

5. Next, implement the `getBitmapFromUri` method:

```
public Bitmap getBitmapFromUri() {
    getContentResolver().notifyChange(mUri, null);
    ContentResolver resolver = getContentResolver();
    Bitmap bitmap;
    try {
        bitmap = android.provider.MediaStore.Images.Media.
getBitmap(
            resolver, mUri);
        return bitmap;
    }
```

```
    catch (Exception e) {
        Toast.makeText(this, e.getMessage(),
         Toast.LENGTH_SHORT).show();
        return null;
    }
}
```

6. Add the appropriate permission and feature to the `AndroidManifest.xml` file:

```
<uses-permission android:name="android.permission.CAMERA" />
<uses-permission
  android:name="android.permission.READ_EXTERNAL_STORAGE"/>
<uses-feature android:name="android.hardware.camera" />
```

7. Now let's implement the `submitEntry` method. We will return the comment and `uri` of the picture and end the activity:

```
private void submitEntry(){
    EditText editComment =   (EditText)
      findViewById(R.id.entry_edit_text_comment);
    Intent intent = new Intent();
    intent.putExtra("comments", editComment.getText().toString());
    if (mUri != null) {
        intent.putExtra("uri", "file://" +
            mUri.getPath().toString());
    }
    setResult(Activity.RESULT_OK, intent);
    finish();
}
```

8. Add the implementation for the `onClick` event of the `add` button. Just call the `submitEntry` method:

```
findViewById(R.id.entry_button_add).setOnClickListener(new View.
OnClickListener() {
    @Override
    public void onClick(View v) {
        submitEntry();
    }
});
```

9. In the `MainActivity` class, we will handle the returned result by overriding the `onActivityResult` method. A new drink will be created and added to the list of drinks. Finally, we will notify the adapter that there is an update to be displayed by adding the following snippet:

```
@Override
protected void onActivityResult(int requestCode, int resultCode,
Intent data) {
    super.onActivityResult(requestCode, resultCode, data);
```

```
        if (requestCode == REQUEST_NEW_ENTRY &&
            resultCode == RESULT_OK) {
            Bundle bundle = data.getExtras();
            Drink newDrink = new Drink();
            newDrink.comments = bundle.getString("comments");
            newDrink.imageUri = bundle.getString("uri");
            newDrink.dateAndTime = new Date();
            mDrinks.add(newDrink);
            mAdapter.notifyDataSetChanged();
    }
```

10. In the `MainAdapter` class, we need to do some work to display thumbnails of each image. Add this to the end of the `onBindViewHolder` method:

```
if (currentDrink.imageUri != null){
    Bitmap bitmap =
     getBitmapFromUri(Uri.parse(currentDrink.imageUri));
    holder.mImageView.setImageBitmap(bitmap);
}
```

11. If an `Uri` is known for the item, we need to display a thumbnail for it. We will implement `getBitmapFromUri` in `MainAdapter` slightly different. The method to do so goes like this:

```
public Bitmap getBitmapFromUri(Uri uri) {
    mContext.getContentResolver().notifyChange(uri, null);
    ContentResolver cr = mContext.getContentResolver();
    try {
        Bitmap bitmap =
android.provider.MediaStore.Images.Media.getBitmap(cr, uri);
        return bitmap;
    }
    catch (Exception e) {
        Toast.makeText(mContext, e.getMessage(),
         Toast.LENGTH_SHORT).show();
        return null;
    }
}
```

Now, run the app. You can use a real device or Genymotion for that. If you are using Genymotion you have to enable the camera, as described in *Chapter 1, Welcome to Android Studio*. Click on the **add** button, have a glass of water, enter some comments, and then take a selfie. Hit the **Add entry** button to make it appear in the list.

This is amazing! You are done for now. The app is far from pixel perfect but we have made some interesting moves. Beautification takes time. In the next recipe, we are going to implement some wow stuff by adding transitions.

On some devices, but not all of them, the picture may be rotated. This is one of the challenges that come with Android development and we will cover that topic in *Chapter 6, Capture and Share*.

There's more...

The list with entries is not yet persisting other than during the life time of the application. If you want, you can make the entries persistent, for example, by storing the entries in a SQLite database or eventually by using Parse, which is discussed in *Chapter 2, Applications with a Cloud-based Backend*. Since persistency is not the objective for this recipe, it will not be discussed any further here. In *Chapter 7, Content providers and observers*, SQLite and content providers are discussed.

 Since API level 23 there is a FloatingActionButton widget that you can use as well. It comes in two sizes: default and mini.

See also

► *Chapter 2, Applications with a Cloud-based Backend*

► *Chapter 6, Capture and Share*

► *Chapter 7, Content providers and observers*

Great transitions

If you click on any of the cards it will display the entry view again with the comments and a preview of the picture that we took previously.

We do not just want to move from the list view to the detail view. Material design also takes care of great natural transitions. This recipe is going to apply just that.

Getting ready

To go through this recipe, you will need to have the previous recipes up and running. This recipe is going to add some animations to it.

How to do it...

The following steps will help us to add the animations to our app:

1. Add a mDrink member to ViewHolder in the MainAdapter class:

```
public Drink mDrink;
```

2. In the same file in the onBindViewHolder method inform the view holder about the actual drink, just after the initialization of currentDrink:

```
Drink currentDrink = mDrinks.get(position);
holder.mDrink = currentDrink;
```

3. In the onCreateViewHolder method, add an OnClickListener to the end:

```
v.setTag(viewHolder);
v.setOnClickListener(new View.OnClickListener() {
    @Override
    public void onClick(View view) {
        ViewHolder holder = (ViewHolder) view.getTag();
        if (view.getId() == holder.itemView.getId())
        {
        }
    }
});
```

4. If the view is being clicked on, we want the EntryActivity class to display the selected drink entry. In order to be able to inform the entry about the selection, we need to make the Drink model a parcelable class:

```
public class Drink implements Parcelable
```

5. We need to implement a couple of methods for that:

```
@Override
public int describeContents() {
    return 0;
}
@Override
public void writeToParcel(Parcel out, int flags) {
    out.writeLong(dateAndTime.getTime());
    out.writeString(comments);
    out.writeString(imageUri);
}
public static final Parcelable.Creator<Drink> CREATOR = new
  Parcelable.Creator<Drink>() {
    public Drink createFromParcel(Parcel in) {
        return new Drink(in);
    }
```

```
        public Drink[] newArray(int size) {
            return new Drink[size];
        }
    };
```

6. Add two constructors for the `Drink` class—a default one and one that takes a parcel—so we can recreate the object and populate it with the appropriate values:

```
public Drink(){
}
public Drink(Parcel in) {
    dateAndTime = new Date(in.readLong());
    comments = in.readString();
    imageUri = in.readString();
}
```

7. In the `MainAdapter` class, add a private variable for the request. This approach makes your code more readable:

```
private int REQUEST_EDIT_ENTRY = 2;
```

The so-called magical numbers are easy to misunderstand and should be avoided as much as possible. This and other recipes are just for demo purposes but in the real world, you should use self-explaining constants where possible. Here, `REQUEST_EDIT_ENTRY` makes much more sense than just putting the number 2 in your code somewhere.

8. Now within the `onClick` method that we created previously in the `onCreateViewHolder` method of the `MainAdapter`, we can start a new entry activity and pass the selected drink as a parameter. The implementation of the `onClick` method will now look like this:

```
v.setOnClickListener(new View.OnClickListener() {
    @Override
    public void onClick(View view) {
        ViewHolder holder = (ViewHolder) view.getTag();
        if (view.getId() == holder.itemView.getId()) {
            Intent intent = new Intent(mContext,
             EntryActivity.class);
            intent.putExtra("edit_drink", holder.mDrink);
    ((Activity)mContext).startActivityForResult(intent,
            REQUEST_EDIT_ENTRY); }
    }
});
```

9. In the `onCreate` method of the `EntryActivity` class, we will retrieve and display the properties of the selected drink. Add this implementation to the end of the method:

```
Intent intent = getIntent();
if (intent.hasExtra("edit_drink")) {
    Drink editableDrink = intent.getParcelableExtra("edit_drink");
    EditText editComment =
      (EditText)findViewById(R.id.entry_edit_text_comment);
    editComment.setText(editableDrink.comments);
    if (editableDrink.imageUri != null) {
        mUri = Uri.parse(editableDrink.imageUri);
        Bitmap bitmap = getBitmapFromUri();
        ImageView preview = (ImageView)
          findViewById(R.id.entry_image_view_preview);
        preview.setImageBitmap(bitmap);
    }
}
```

The EditText for the comments will be filled with the comments so that the user can edit them. If an image is attached to the drink entry, it will be shown in the preview image view. Now if only we had an easy and cool way of animating the thumbnail of the image into the preview:

1. Surprise! There is. Add a new string resource in the `strings.xml` (in the `res/values` folder) file:

```
<string name="transition_preview">transition_preview
  </string>
```

2. In the `onCreateViewHolder` method in the `MainAdapter` class, within the `onClick` implementation, and right before the `startActivityForResult` method, we will use the `ActivityOptionsCompat` class to create a transition from the thumbnail (the holder's `mImageView` member) to the preview image in the layout for the entry activity:

```
ActivityOptionsCompat options =
 ActivityOptionsCompat.makeSceneTransitionAnimation(
   ((Activity)mContext), holder.mImageView,
    mContext.getString (R.string.transition_preview));
```

3. Supply these options by replacing the `startActivityForResult` call on the next line with this implementation:

```
ActivityCompat.startActivityForResult(((Activity) mContext),
 intent, REQUEST_EDIT_ENTRY, options.toBundle());
```

4. Open the `adapter_main_card_view.xml` layout file and add this line to the image view (the one with the `main_image_view` ID):

```
android:transitionName="@string/transition_preview"
```

5. In the `activity_entry.xml` layout, add this line as well to the `ImageView` widget (the one with the `entry_image_view_preview` ID). This way Android knows where the transition of the thumbnail into the larger preview image has to go).

 It is good practice to use string resources. We can use these resources here to make sure we are talking about the same transition everywhere in the code but it will also be great for localization purposes.

Now if you run your app and click on any of the cards in the `MainActivity` class, you will see that the thumbnail is enlarged and fits into the place holder for the preview image in the layout of the `EntryActivity` class. The reversed transition is shown if you choose the back button. In previous versions we could not do this with only a few lines of code!

Theming

As a bonus, let's do some theming using the following steps:

1. Visit `http://www.materialpalette.com` and pick two colors. Theming comes up with a color set that we can use for a theme as shown in the following screenshot:

2. Create a `color.xml` file in the `res/values` folder and add the suggested color names and values. I have chosen blue and indigo on the website so my color resource file looks like this:

```xml
<?xml version="1.0" encoding="utf-8"?>
<resources>
    <color name="primary_dark">#1976d2</color>
    <color name="primary">#2193f3</color>
    <color name="light_primary">#bbdefb</color>
    <color name="text">#ffffff</color>
    <color name="accent">#536dfe</color>
    <color name="primary_text">#212121</color>
    <color name="secondary_text">#727272</color>
    <color name="divider_color">#b6b6b6</color>
</resources>
```

3. Edit the `styles.xml` file in the `res/values` folder and make it look like this:

```xml
<resources>
    <style name="AppTheme" parent="Theme.AppCompat.Light">
        <item name="android:colorPrimary">@color/primary</item>
        <item name="android:colorPrimaryDark">@color/primary_dark
        /item>
        <item name="android:colorAccent">@color/accent</item>
        <item name="android:textColor">@color/text</item>
        <item name="android:textColorPrimary">@color/primary_text
        </item>
      <item name="android:textColorSecondary">
         @color/secondary_text
      </item>
    </style>
</resources>
```

The output of the preceding code is as shown in the following screenshot:

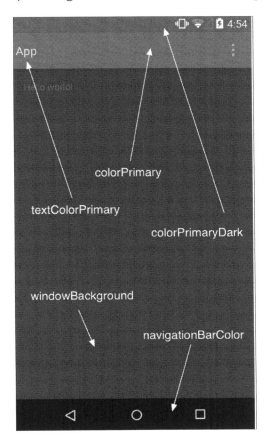

4. Modify your layout files and change text views and other elements so that it can reflect the color scheme. Run the app.

How it works...

Android's activity transitions will take care of everything. We just need to tell what, where, and how. With just a few lines of code the API allows you to create meaningful transitions between activities, which will heavily improve the **User Experience** (**UX**) of your application.

With each new step, the looks of your app become better and better! Unfortunately, this is where this introduction to material design ends. Make improvements wherever you want. Play with it and have fun! Animations, UX, and layouts are important elements of high-quality apps.

For wearable apps, this may be even more important as we will see in the next chapter. But how can we enable a great user experience on such as small screen?

There's more...

We have seen only a few aspects of Material Design. There is so much more to discover.

Improve the looks and UX of the app further, add the implementation in the `MainActivity` class to handle the data of drink entries that you have added, and make enhancements wherever you want them. Or, you can have a look at your existing apps and see how you can materialize them.

4

Android Wear

This chapter will inform you about Android Wear and how the phenomenon materializes as watches and other devices.

In this chapter, you will learn about:

- ▶ Wearables
- ▶ A fullscreen wearable app
- ▶ Watch faces
- ▶ Notifications

Wearables

Android Wear is what many wearable devices run on. You might have a smartwatch yourself. Will wearables be the next hype after phones, phablets, and tablets? Or will smartwatches become part of something bigger, such as the **Internet of Things (IoT)**?

Android Wear is a special version of the Android SDK and is dedicated to wearables that are often more limited in hardware and available sensors and have smaller screens. Wearables may appear as watches, glasses, or maybe in future as contact lenses, tattoos, or clothing.

Currently, we see wearables appearing mostly as watches but there are plenty of other wearable devices that you can think of. However, it will take some time for people to adopt this new technology. Think of the Google Glass project for example. It is a brilliant solution but mostly because of the built-in camera, people are having serious objections to it. In San Francisco, they have even made up a word for it: glass hole. Hmm. That is not really flattering is it? Let's have a look at the following device:

Devices do not necessarily have to be wearable. When the IOT is discussed, project Brillo comes to mind. It extends the Android platform to any connected device that you can think of. In future, Brillo and Android Wear might even be merged.

Imagine a hot summer day; the fridge notifies us about the fact that we are running out of sparkling water (or was it beer?). Cool! The learning thermostat sets the temperature to 18°C an hour before you come home. Even cooler! The light in the living room dims automatically because it is late in the evening; you are playing some romantic music and the system knows you have just opened a bottle of wine-Ehrm. Weird. That is a completely different story and so is Brillo for now.

Instead, let's find out which apps we can build for a smart watch such as a brand new watch face or a health app displaying notifications from time to time. In the upcoming recipes, we will see what we need to do for that.

First things first, let's see if we can get things up and running on a wearable device. For the first two recipes, you do not need to have a real smartwatch. We will create a virtual one in the first recipe.

Fullscreen wearable app

Wearable fullscreen apps do have a phone (or other handheld device) and a wearable component. The user install the handheld app on their phone and the wearable component is pushed to the paired wear device automatically.

This is a great start to exploring the interesting world of developing apps for wearables, as they are basically the same as Android phone apps. However, Google encourages you to integrate your app with Android Wear's context stream. This context stream does contain various interesting pieces of information. Think of them as incoming e-mails, the weather, the number of steps you have taken today, or your heart beat rate. We will find out more about this in the recipe about notifications.

Getting ready

To go through this recipe, you need to have Android Studio up and running. Also make sure that you have installed the latest SDK, including the Android Wear SDK. You can check whether this is the case when you open the SDK manager. (Navigate to the **Tools** menu, **Android SDK Manager**) as shown in the following screenshot:

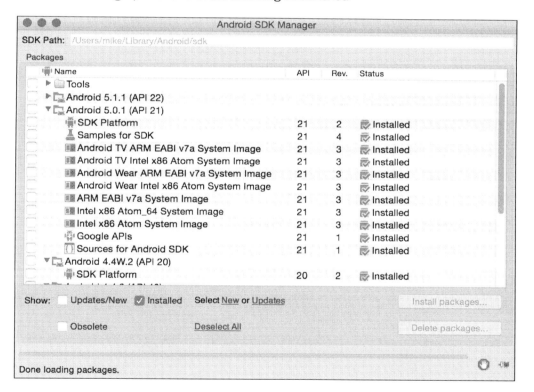

How to do it...

Let's see how we can create our own wearable app and make it run on a virtual device using the following steps:

1. Start a new Android Studio project. Name your application `WatchApp` and enter `packtpub.com` in the **Company Domain** field. Then, click on the **Next** button.

2. In the next dialog, check **Phone and tablet**. Also check the **Wear** option.

3. For both options, select **API 21** or higher and click on the **Next** button.

4. In the **Add an activity to wear** dialog, choose **Blank Wear Activity** and click on the **Next** button.

5. Select **Blank Activity** and click on the **Next** button.

6. Name your new activity `PhoneActivity` and click on the **Next** button.

7. Select **Blank Wear Activity** and click on the **Next** button as shown in the following screenshot:

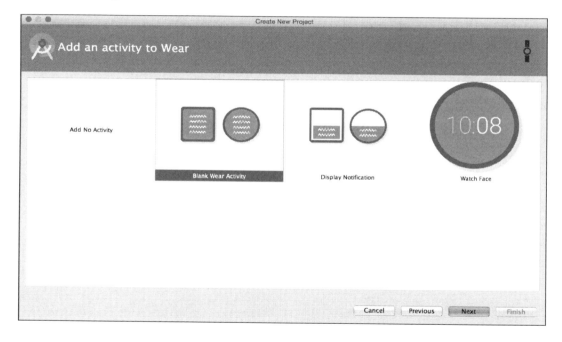

8. Name your new wear activity `WatchActivity` and click on the **Finish** button.

9. Android Studio will create two modules: `mobile` and `wear`. The mobile one runs on a smartphone (or phablet or tablet). The wear app will be pushed to a paired wearable device such as your smart watch for example. The project view now looks like this:

10. Let's see what it will look like on a smartphone by default. To do so, we will create a wearable virtual device. From the **Tools** menu, select the **Android** option and next select the **AVD Manager** option.

11. Then, click on the button that reads **Create virtual device**.

12. In the dialog that comes up, choose **Wear** in the **Category** list. Choose the **Android Wear Round** device in the list next to it and click on the **Next** button as shown in the following screenshot:

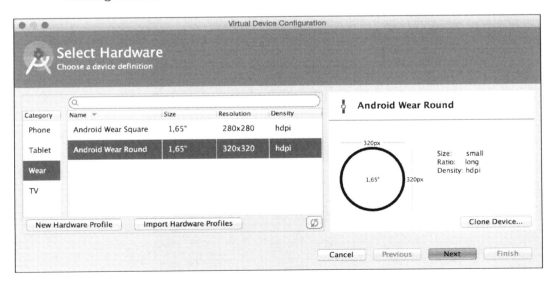

13. In the next dialog, choose a system image, for example **Lollipop**, **API level 21**, **x86** (or higher if available. You might need to click on the **Download** link first to do so). Then, click on the **Next** button to continue.

14. Give your virtual device a nice name and click on the **Finish** button. Your new Android wear device will now appear in the list as shown in the next screenshot:

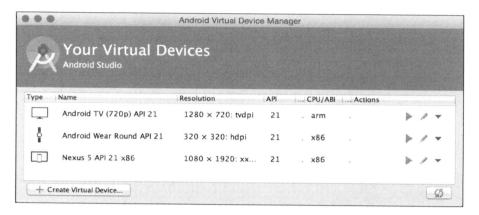

15. Start the device by clicking on the play icon.

16. Once the virtual device has been booted, change the configuration to **wear** and click on the **Run** button next to it on the toolbar.

After the app has been installed, it will look like this:

If the **Hello Round World!** message does not appear immediately, the app may have been installed but may not be visible yet. Swipe the screen a couple of times to check whether it is there.

If your app is up and running, it is time to explore something that is even more fun. Let's create a watch face in the next recipe.

There's more...

At the time of writing this, Genymotion does not support wearable devices yet. This is why we are using the default emulator instead in this recipe.

But that one is so slooooow! You might say. That is true, but by installing HAXM, you can make it a little bit faster. There is some interesting information about this topic at `http://developer.android.com/tools/devices/emulator.html`.

In case you do have a real device, you can of course also deploy your app on a smartwatch. If you want to do so, you also need to have the Android wear companion app installed on a handheld device since you cannot install and test your wearable app on it directly.

You can get this companion app from Google Play. Download the app, install it, and connect your handheld device through a USB.

See also

- ▶ Refer *Testing your app with an emulator called Genymotion* section from *Chapter 1, Welcome to Android Studio*

Watch faces

Out of the box, your Android smartwatch comes with various watch faces and there are plenty of other watch faces that you can download. They are available in any shape or type: square and round or analogue and digital. Actually, there is even another shape - the so-called flat tire one - as seen on the Moto 360 device.

There are many customization options that you can think of but all watch faces are about displaying time and date information in an easy way. This is what watches are for in the first place, aren't they?

They should be aware of incoming notifications and also need to make room for the system indicators such as the battery life icon and the **Ok Google** text. For more information, check out `https://developer.android.com/design/wear/watchfaces.html`.

What we will create in the upcoming recipe is a watch face that tells you the time, for example, **half past seven** or **five minutes past ten**.

Getting ready

To go through this recipe, you need to have Android Studio up and running. Also make sure you have installed the latest SDK, including the Android Wear SDK. You can check whether this is the case by opening the SDK manager, which is accessible when you navigate to the **Tools** menu under **Android** which is under the **SDK Manager** menu item.

How to do it...

Let's create a new Android project with the following steps to create a watch face app:

1. Create a new Android Studio project.
2. Name your app `HelloTime` or whatever you want the name of your app to be. Enter `packtpub.com` in the **Company Domain** field. Then click on the **Next** button.
3. In the next dialog, check **Phone and tablet**. Also check the **Wear** option.
4. For both options, select **API 21** or a higher version and click on the **Next** button.
5. Select **Blank activity** and click on the **Next** button.
6. Name your new activity `PhoneActivity` and click on the **Next** button.
7. Select **Watch Face** and click on the **Next** button.
8. Name the watch face `HelloTimeWatchFace` and choose **Digital** for **Style**. After that, click on the **Finish** button.
9. Android Studio will create the necessary modules for both the phone or tablet and the wearable device.
10. In the project view, open the `HelloTimeWatchFace` class of the `wear` module.
11. Open the `strings.xml` file in the `res/values` folder within the `wear` module and change the string for `my_digital_name` to `Hello Time!`
12. Let's see what we have got so far. Start the virtual (or your real) wearable device. In case you do not know how to create a virtual wearable device, refer to the previous recipe.
13. Once the virtual device has been booted, change the configuration to **Wear** and click on the **Run** button next to it on the toolbar as shown in the following figure:

14. On the wearable, swipe to see the **Settings** icon and click on it.
15. Swipe down to **Change watch face** and click on it.
16. Swipe to the right until you see the **Hello Time!** watch face and click on it.
17. You will now see the digital watch face that Android Studio has created for you.

Let's examine this code for a bit. The `HelloTimeWatchFace` class that has been created for you extends `CanvasWatchFaceService` and an inner `Engine` class has been added. The engine has a handler so that the time could be updated. It also has a broadcast receiver that will handle the situation if the user moves to another time zone while traveling.

The `Engine` class has some interesting methods. The `onCreate` method allocates two `Paint` objects: one for the background and one for the foreground (text). The `onVisibilityChanged` method will be called when the user displays or hides the watch face. The `onApplyWindowInSets` method is used to determine whether the app is running on a round or square screen.

Next there is the `onPropertiesChanged` method, which will be called once the hardware properties of the wearable device are known, for example, if the low-bit ambient mode is supported. The `onAmbientModeChanged` method is very important because it can save the battery. It can also be used to apply burn-in protection. Here you may want to change the color of the background or foreground.

Let's change the way the time is shown:

1. Add a method that returns the current time in the spoken language, something like this:

```
private String[] getFullTextTime(){
    String time = "";
    Calendar cal = Calendar.getInstance();
    int minute = cal.get(Calendar.MINUTE);
    int hour = cal.get(Calendar.HOUR);
    if (minute<=7){
        time = String.format("%s o'clock",
         getTextDigit(hour));
    }
    else if (minute<=15){
        time = String.format("ten past %s",
         getTextDigit(hour));
    }
    else if (minute<=25){
        time = String.format("Quarter past %s",
         getTextDigit(hour));
    }
    else if (minute<=40){
        time = String.format("Half past %s",
        getTextDigit(hour));
    }
    else if (minute<53){
        time = String.format("Quarter to %s",
```

```
            getTextDigit(hour));
    }
    else {
        time = String.format("Almost %d o'clock",
        (hour<=11)? hour+1: 1);
    }
    return time.split(" ");
}
```

2. Add this method to convert the numbers to text:

```
private String getTextDigit(int digit){
    String[] texts ={ "twelve", "one", "two", "three",
     "four", "five", "six", "seven", "eight", "nine",
        "eleven"};
    return texts[digit];
```

3. In the onDraw method, replace the canvas.DrawText part with the lines shown here. This method displays multiple lines of the current time in the spoken language:

```
String[] timeTextArray = getFullTextTime();
float y = mYOffset;
for (String timeText : timeTextArray){
    canvas.drawText(timeText, mXOffset, y, mTextPaint);
    y+=65;
}
```

Magic is not always cool...

Wait! What is that magic number doing there in the previous step? 65 is not really meaningful. What does this mean? What does it do? Create a constant value for it somewhere in your class and use that variable name instead (here it would be even better to put the value in a dimension resource file, but we will have a look at that later so let's forget about that for now):

```
    private static final int ROW_HEIGHT  = 65;
    y+= ROW_HEIGHT;
```

4. Go to the onCreate method and add this line to make the text appear with a nice green color (yep, GREEN is a constant as well):

```
mTextPaint.setColor(Color.GREEN);
```

Run your app again. It will look like this:

To prepare the watch face for the Play Store later, you need to take screenshots once you have completed it. You need to provide screenshots for both square and circular watches. In the `res/drawable` folder, you will find the default preview images that Android Studio has created for you.

For now, you have just created your first watch face app in its most basic shape. In the next recipe, we will see what happens when a notification comes in.

There's more...

The watch face app in this recipe is far from perfect. The text is not aligned; it does not properly respond to ambient mode changes and you may want to localize it to display the time in your own language.

To see where this could be going, you could check out the many watch faces that are already available at the Play Store.

Notifications

Android Wear is somewhat different from apps running on phones or tablets. Instead of icons and lists, Android Wear uses cards, which is something we saw already in the recipes that introduced us to the basic concepts of material design.

According to the context and only at a relevant moment, a card is added to the stream of cards once a new notification arrives. This is known as the context stream, and it does contain various interesting pieces of information. Think of them as incoming emails, the weather, the number of steps you took today, your heart beat rate, and other events or reminders.

Remember the water app from the previous chapter? For example, we could create a notification to remind us to drink water more often and to add a new card for it. This would be a nice feature to have.

Getting ready

This recipe requires Android Studio and the latest SDKs, including the wear SDK, installed. Check out the previous recipe for more information.

You also need a handheld device running on Android Lollipop or above that has the `Android Wear` app installed and a wearable device that is connected to your handheld device through Bluetooth.

How to do it...

Let's see how notifications can be triggered and how to display them nicely on a smartwatch:

1. Create a new project in Android Studio. Name it `WaterNowNotification` and click on the **Next** button.
2. Choose **Phone and Tablet** as smartwatch platform. Do not check the **Wear** option. Click on the **Next** button.
3. Select **Blank Activity** and click on the **Next** button.
4. Name your activity `WaterNowActivity` and click on the **Finish** button.
5. Open the `build.gradle` file in your app. Add this to the dependencies section and apply the appropriate version for it:

    ```
    compile 'com.android.support:support-v4:22.0+'
    ```

6. Click on the **Sync project with Gradle files** button that you can find on the toolbar.
7. Open the `activity_water_now.xml` file and change it to the **Text** mode using the tab at the bottom of Android Studio.
8. Create a layout with a button that we will use to send a test notification:

    ```
    <LinearLayout
    xmlns:android="http://schemas.android.com/apk/res/android"
    xmlns:tools="http://schemas.android.com/tools"
    android:layout_width="match_parent"
    android:layout_height="match_parent"
    android:orientation="vertical"
    tools:context=".WaterNowActivity">
    ```

```
<Button
android:layout_width="wrap_content"
android:layout_height="wrap_content"
android:text="Drink water now!"
android:id="@+id/water_now_button"
android:layout_gravity="center" />
</LinearLayout>
```

9. In the `onCreate` method of the `WaterNowActivity` class, add an `onClick` handler for the button that we just created. Use the *Alt + Enter* shortcut to add import statements as needed:

```
Button waterNowButton = (Button)findViewById(R.id.water_now_
button);
waterNowButton.setOnClickListener(new View.OnClickListener() {
@Override
public void onClick(View v) {
      sendNotification();
   }
});
```

10. Create the `sendNotification` method:

```
private void sendNotification(){
    NotificationCompat.Builder notificationBuilder =
    new NotificationCompat.Builder(
      WaterNowActivity.this)
      .setContentTitle("Water app!")
      .setSmallIcon(R.drawable.icon)
      .setContentText("Hey there! Drink water now!");
    NotificationManagerCompat notificationManager =
     NotificationManagerCompat.from(
      WaterNowActivity.this);
    notificationManager.notify(1 ,
     notificationBuilder.build());
}
```

11. Notifications do require an icon, so create one in the `res/drawable` folder. Create a drawable `icon.xml` file and add the implementation to create a nice blue circle:

```
<?xml version="1.0" encoding="utf-8"?>
<shape xmlns:android= "http://schemas.android.com/apk/res/android"
android:shape="oval">
<corners android:radius="10dip"/>
<stroke android:color="#0000FF" android:width="15dip"/>
<solid android:color="#0000FF"/>
</shape>
```

12. Connect your handheld device; make sure that the wearable device is connected (use the `Android wear` app to check this) and run the app. You will see the output similar to the following screenshot:

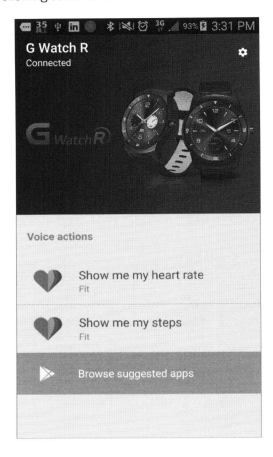

13. Click on the **Drink water now** button within your app.

14. A notification will be shown on your phone similar to the following screenshot. If it does not appear right away, there will be some indicator at the top of the screen. In this case, open the notification center to see it.

15. If all is up and running and configured correctly, the same notification appears on the wearable device, shown as follows:

16. If notifications are shown on your phone but do not appear on your wearable, then verify the **Notification access** settings. Open the **Settings** app and choose **Sound and messages**. Next, choose **Notification access** and check whether the **Android Wear** option has been checked.

For other Android versions or for particular brands (customized Android versions), the setting you are looking for may be located elsewhere and/or may have a different name.

There's more...

Where to go from here? You can combine this notification recipe with the Water app from the recipes within the *Chapter 3, Material Design* and create something cooler or you can check whether you can find a way to customize the notification.

Smartwatches, phones, phablets, and tablets come with screens of all sizes and shapes. How can we benefit from a larger screen or how can we provide smart navigations for smaller screens and maintain the same functionality and code within one app?

Different layouts for different Android versions? Multiple layouts are what we need combined with multiple fragments. This is where the recipes in the next chapter come in.

See also

▶ Refer to the *RecyclerView and CardView* section from *Chapter 3, Material Design*

▶ Refer to *Chapter 5, Size does matter*

5
Size Does Matter

This chapter is about building apps that will be running on a wide variety of devices: phones, phablets, tablets, and TVs. We will connect to YouTube to get some data and videos to display.

Size and context actually do matter. We could of course scale up everything but that does not really make it a better app. Tablets offer more space than phones, and when it comes to user interaction, TV differs from a smart phone. How do we make the layout scale and look smooth on each device? How do we find the right approach for each type of device?

In this chapter, you will learn from the following recipes:

- ▶ Size and context
- ▶ Phone, phablet, and tablet layouts
- ▶ Media playback
- ▶ TV and media centre

Size and context

Devices such as phones, phablets, tablets, and TVs come with screens of all sizes and shapes. How can we benefit from a larger screen or how can we provide smart navigation for smaller screens and maintain the same functionality and code within one app? That is what this first recipe is about.

What about the various kinds of devices? With the introduction of wearable devices, we saw that the user behavior for these types of devices is quite different. The same thing applies to TVs. As always, let's do first things first. Let's examine an app that runs on both a phone and tablet.

Phone, phablet, and tablet

A well-known pattern for phones is the list or the recycler view that show you some details when you click on any of the rows. On a small screen, the app will navigate you to a different view. This pattern simply exists because of the lack of space on the screen of a phone. If you run the same app on a device that has sufficient space, we can show the list on the left-hand side of the screen and the details on the right-hand side.

Multiple layouts are what we need, combined with multiple fragments. If we do this, we can reduce the amount of code we need to write. We just do not want to repeat ourselves, do we?

Fragments are a powerful but also an often misunderstood component of Android development. Fragments are (little) pieces of functionality and most of the time do have their own layouts. Using fragment containers, a fragment may reside in multiple places and on multiple activity-related layouts. This is how we can reuse functionality and layouts.

Fragments should be used carefully though. Without a proper strategy, an app that uses fragments can cause you a lot of trouble. Code within a fragment frequently refers to an activity. While this code may still be running, the fragment may be detached from the activity in between (for example, because the user has pressed the back button). This could result in a crash of your app.

Getting ready

To go through this recipe, you need to have Android Studio up and running, and a phone, phablet, and/or tablet device (physical ones are recommended as always; however, you can use Genymotion to create virtual ones).

Since we will be using the YouTube Android API, you need to have the latest YouTube Android app installed on your device as well. Check on your device whether it is there, or install or update it using the Google Play app in case it is not on your device or an update for it is available.

Finally, you need to have a developer's account. In case you do not have one yet, you need to create one first from `http://developer.android.com/distribute/ googleplay/ start.html`.

In addition to buying this book, getting yourself a developer's account is a very good investment, and I strongly recommend you to get one. You will need one in order to be able to submit your app to the Google Play store anyway!

How to do it...

Let's see how we can create our own wearable app and make it run on a device:

1. Start a new Android Studio project. Name your application `YouTubeMediaApp` and enter `packt.com` in the **Company Domain** field. Click on the **Next** button.

2. In the following dialog, only check the **Phone and Tablet** option and click on the **Next** button.

3. In the next dialog, choose **Blank activity** and click on the **Next** button.

4. In the **Customize the Activity** dialog, click on the **Finish** button.

5. Android Studio will create the new project for you. From the **Project** view on the left-hand side of Android Studio, locate `build.gradle` within the `app` folder and open it.

6. Open the `build.gradle` file within the `app` folder and add a dependency to the `dependencies` section for the YouTube services API. We are going to use this API to search for videos on YouTube:

    ```
    compile 'com.google.apis:google-api-services-
    youtube:v3-rev120-1.19.0'
    ```

7. Synchronize the project (click on the **Sync now** link or use the **Sync project with Gradle files** button from the toolbar).

8. Open the `activity_main.xml` layout. Create a frame layout that will act as a container for the fragment that we want to display here later. We will give it a nice background color for demonstration purposes. Let's pick orange:

    ```
    <?xml version="1.0" encoding="utf-8"?>
    <FrameLayout xmlns:android=
      "http://schemas.android.com/apk/res/android"
        android:layout_width="match_parent"
        android:layout_height="match_parent"
        android:background="@android:color/holo_orange_light"
        android:id="@+id/main_container_for_list_fragment">
    </FrameLayout>
    ```

9. Add a new layout and name it `fragment_list.xml`. Create a list view within a container. This list will contain the title and other information about the videos that we will find on YouTube:

    ```
    <?xml version="1.0" encoding="utf-8"?>
    <FrameLayout xmlns:android=
      "http://schemas.android.com/apk/res/android"
        android:orientation="vertical"
        android:layout_width="match_parent"
        android:layout_height="match_parent">
    ```

```
<ListView
    android:id="@+id/main_video_list_view"
    android:visibility="visible"
    android:padding="6dp"
    android:layout_marginTop="0dp"
    android:layout_width="match_parent"
    android:layout_height="match_parent">
</ListView>
</FrameLayout>
```

10. Add a new Java class, name it `ListFragment`, and click on the **OK** button to continue.

11. Make the new class a `Fragment` descendant and override the `onCreate` method. Create a private member for the list view and add a reference to the list view in the layout as shown in the following code:

```
public class ListFragment extends Fragment {
  private ListView mListView;
  @Override
  public View onCreateView(LayoutInflater inflater,
   ViewGroup container, Bundle savedInstanceState)
    final View view= inflater.inflate(
       R.layout.fragment_list, container, false);
    mListView = (ListView)view.findViewById(
     R.id.main_video_list_view);
    return view;
  }
}
```

 Besides `ListActivity`, there is also a `ListFragment` class that you can descend from. For demo purposes, we will descend from `Fragment` class here and do some things ourselves.

12. While adding the correct import statements (using the *Alt + Enter* shortcut or otherwise) you will be able to choose which package to import. You can choose between the `android.app.Fragment` and `android.support.v4.app. Fragment` packages. The last one is for backward compatibility purposes only. Since we will be using the latest SDK for our app, choose this import statement if asked:

```
import android.app.Fragment;
```

13. Add another private member for YouTube and a YouTube list and create a method named `loadVideos`. First, we will initialize the YouTube member:

```
private YouTube mYoutube;
private YouTube.Search.List mYouTubeList;
private void loadVideos(String queryString){
 mYoutube = new YouTube.Builder(new NetHttpTransport(),
  new JacksonFactory(), new HttpRequestInitializer() {
   @Override
   public void initialize(HttpRequest hr) throws
    IOException {}
 }).setApplicationName(
  getString(R.string.app_name)).build();
}
```

14. Next, we will tell YouTube what we are looking for and what information we want the API to return. We need to wrap our code in a try catch construction as we do not know in advance whether we will be able to connect to YouTube. Add this to the end of the `loadVideos` method:

```
try{
 mYouTubeList = mYoutube.search().list("id,snippet");
 mYouTubeList.setType("video");
 mYouTubeList.setFields(
  "items(id/videoId,snippet/title,snippet/
    description,snippet/thumbnails/default/url)");
}
catch (IOException e) {
  Log.d(this.getClass().toString(), "Could not
    initialize: " + e);
}
```

15. To use the YouTube API, you must register your app first. To do so, navigate your browser to `https://console.developers.google.com/project`.

16. Click on the **Create** a project button. Enter `YouTubeApp` as the project name and click on the **Create** button.

17. Once the project is created, the dashboard will be shown on the webpage. On the left-hand side, expand **APIs and auth** and click on **APIs**.

18. On the right-hand side of the page, click on YouTube Data API. Click on the **Enable API** button.

19. On the left-hand side again, click on **Credentials** just after APIs. Under Public API access, click on the **Create new Key** button.

20. On the **Create new key** popup dialog box, click on the **Android key** button.

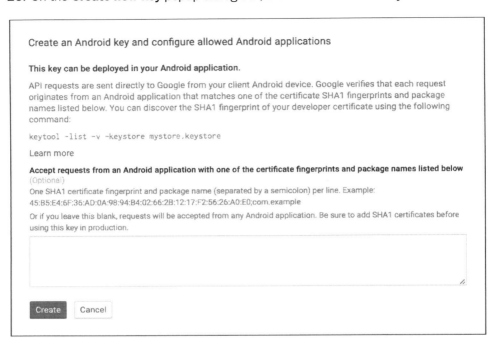

21. Since this app is for demo purposes only, we do not need to look up the requested **SHA1** value. Just click on the **Create** button.

22. Now, an API key will be created for you. Copy the value for API key.

23. In the `AndroidManifest.xml` file, add a permission to access the Internet:

```
android:name="android.permission.INTERNET"/>
```

Glue it together!

1. Now back in the `ListFragment` class, tell the API about your key that is just next to the `search` call on the YouTube object:

```
mYouTubeList.setKey("Your API key goes here");
```

2. Create a new `VideoItem` class and add members to hold the requested information for each video. Note that we are using getters and setters here:

```
private String title;
private String description;
private String thumbnailURL;
private String id;
public String getId() {
  return id;
}
```

```java
public void setId(String id) {
 this.id = id;
}
public String getTitle() {
 return title;
}
public void setTitle(String title) {
 this.title = title;
}
public String getDescription() {
 return description;
}
public void setDescription(String description) {
 this.description = description;
}
public String getThumbnailURL() {
 return thumbnailURL;
}
public void setThumbnailURL(String thumbnail) {
 this.thumbnailURL = thumbnail;
}
```

3. Create a new layout and name it `adapter_video.xml`. Then, add text views to display the video information:

```xml
<?xml version="1.0" encoding="utf-8"?>
<LinearLayout android:layout_width="match_parent"
  android:layout_height="wrap_content"
  android:orientation="vertical"
   xmlns:android=
     "http://schemas.android.com/apk/res/android"
  android:padding="6dp">
<TextView
  android:id="@+id/adapter_video_id"
  android:textSize="14sp"
  android:textStyle="bold"
  android:layout_width="match_parent"
  android:layout_height="wrap_content" />
<TextView
  android:id="@+id/adapter_video_title"
  android:textSize="20sp"
  android:layout_marginTop="2dp"
  android:layout_width="match_parent"
  android:layout_height="wrap_content" />
</LinearLayout>
```

4. Create a new `VideoAdapter` class and make it an `ArrayAdapter` descendant that
    will be holding entries of the `VideoItem` type. A view holder will help us fill the text
    views with the properties of the listed `VideoItem` object:

```java
public class VideoAdapter extends ArrayAdapter<VideoItem> {
 private Context mContext;
 private int mAdapterResourceId;
 public ArrayList<VideoItem>mVideos = null;
 static class ViewHolder{
        TextView videoId;
        TextView videoTitle;
     }
@Override
public int getCount(){
 super.getCount();
 int count = mVideos !=null ? mVideos.size() : 0;
 return count;
}
public VideoAdapter (Context context, int
 adapterResourceId, ArrayList<VideoItem> items)
{
 super(context, adapterResourceId, items);
 this.mVideos = items;
 this.mContext = context;
 this.mAdapterResourceId = adapterResourceId;
}
@Override
public View getView(int position, View convertView, ViewGroup
parent)
{
 View v = convertView;
if (v == null){
    LayoutInflater vi =
      (LayoutInflater)this.getContext().getSystemService(
      Context.LAYOUT_INFLATER_SERVICE);
    v = vi.inflate(mAdapterResourceId, null);
    ViewHolder holder = new ViewHolder();
    holder.videoId = (TextView)
     v.findViewById(R.id.adapter_video_id);
    holder.videoTitle = (TextView)
     v.findViewById(R.id.adapter_video_title);

    v.setTag(holder);
}
final VideoItem item = mVideos.get(position);
if(item != null){
```

```
final ViewHolder holder = (ViewHolder)v.getTag();
holder.videoId.setText(item.getId());
holder.videoTitle.setText( item.getTitle());
}
return v;
}
```

5. Now back to the `ListFragment` class. Add two more private members in it, one for the list of videos that we have found and one for the adapter that we have just created:

```
private List<VideoItem>mVideos;
private VideoAdapter mAdapter;
```

6. Add a `search` method to the `ListFragment` class:

```
public List<VideoItem> search(String keywords){
 mYouTubeList.setQ(keywords);
try{
    SearchListResponse response = mYouTubeList.execute();
    List<SearchResult> results = response.getItems();
    List<VideoItem>  items = new ArrayList<VideoItem>();
    for(SearchResult result:results){

    VideoItem item = new VideoItem();
    item.setTitle(result.getSnippet().getTitle());
    item.setDescription(result.getSnippet().
     getDescription());

    item.setThumbnailURL(result.getSnippet().
     getThumbnails().getDefault().getUrl());
    item.setId(result.getId().getVideoId());
    items.add(item);
  }
  return items;
 }
catch(IOException e){
   Log.d("TEST", "Could not search: " + e);
   return null;
  }
}
```

7. Toward the end of the `loadVideos` method, add the implementation to call the `search` method and initialize the adapter:

```
mVideos =search(queryString§);
mAdapter = new VideoAdapter(getActivity(), R.layout.adapter_video,
(ArrayList<VideoItem>) mVideos);
```

8. Tell the list view about the adapter and call the `notifyDataSetChanged` method of the adapter to inform that new entries are available to be shown. For this, we will use a `Runnable` instance that will be running on the UI thread:

```
getActivity().runOnUiThread(new Runnable() {
public void run() {
   mListView.setAdapter(mAdapter);
   mAdapter.notifyDataSetChanged();
  }
});
```

9. Now we will load the video information asynchronously, as we do want the app to be responsive while getting data from the Internet. Create a new thread and call `loadVideos` inside within the `run` method. Let's assume we want to look at *Android development* videos:

```
@Override
public void onActivityCreated(Bundle bundle){
  super.onActivityCreated(bundle);
  new Thread(new Runnable() {
    public void run(){
        loadVideos("Android development");
    }
}).start();
}
```

10. Create a new layout and name it `fragment_details.xml`. In this fragment, we will display a thumbnail and the description of a video that the user has selected from the list. Since we are here anyway, let's add a play button as well. We will need it in the next recipe:

```
<?xml version="1.0" encoding="utf-8"?>
<LinearLayout  xmlns:android=
  "http://schemas.android.com/apk/res/android"
android:orientation="vertical" android:layout_width="match_parent"
android:layout_height="match_parent">
<Button
android:id="@+id/detail_button_play"
android:text="@string/play"
android:layout_width="match_parent"
android:layout_height="wrap_content" />
<ImageView
android:id="@+id/detail_image"
android:layout_width="match_parent"
android:layout_height="wrap_content"
android:src="@android:drawable/gallery_thumb"/>
<TextView
android:layout_marginTop="16dp"
android:id="@+id/detail_text"
```

```
android:minHeight="200dp"
android:layout_width="match_parent"
android:layout_height="wrap_content" />
</LinearLayout>
```

11. Create the `DetailsFragment` class:

```java
public class DetailsFragment  extends Fragment {
  @Override
  public View onCreateView(LayoutInflater inflater,
   ViewGroup container, Bundle savedInstanceState) {
    final View view= inflater.inflate(
      R.layout.fragment_details, container, false);
    return view;
  }
}
```

12. Add the `showDetails` private method to `DetailsFragment` class. In this method, we will set the text for the description and create a new runnable instance to load the thumbnail for the video. Also, add the `setVideo` method and override the `onResume` method:

```java
private void showDetails(){
if (getView()!=null &&mVideo != null)
  {
    TextView tv = (TextView)
     getView().findViewById(R.id.detail_text);
    final ImageView iv = (ImageView)
     getView().findViewById(R.id.detail_image);
    tv.setText(mVideo.getDescription());
   new Thread(new Runnable() {
    public void run() {
       loadThumbnail(mVideo, iv);
     }
    }).start();
  }
}
public void setVideo(VideoItem video)
{
  mVideo = video;
  showDetails();
}
@Override
public void onResume(){
  super.onResume();
  showDetails();
}
```

13. Now, add the `loadThumbnail` method to `DetailsFragment` class and the implementation to load the thumbnail image from the given URL:

```
private void loadThumbnail(VideoItem video,final
  ImageView iv){
try
  {
     URL url = new URL(video.getThumbnailURL());
    final Bitmap bmp = BitmapFactory.decodeStream(
    url.openConnection().getInputStream());

    getActivity().runOnUiThread(new Runnable() {
     public void run() {
       iv.setImageBitmap(bmp);
       }
     });
  }
  catch (Exception ex){
     Log.d(this.getClass().toString(), ex.getMessage());
  }
}
```

14. If the user selects an item from the list view in the `ListFragment` class, we need to tell `DetailFragment` to display the corresponding details. In the `onCreateView` method of the `ListFragment` class, add the onItemClick handler:

```
mListView.setOnItemClickListener(new
  AdapterView.OnItemClickListener()
{
  @Override
  public void onItemClick(AdapterView<?> adapterView,
    View view, int i, long l)
    {
        VideoItem video = mVideos.get(i);
        onVideoClicked(video);
    }
});
return view;
```

15. In the `MainActivity` class, add two static members that will represent the tags for both the `ListFragment` and `DetailsFragment` classes:

```
public static String TAG_LIST_FRAGMENT = "LIST";
public static String TAG_DETAILS_FRAGMENT = "DETAILS";
```

16. Create the `onVideoClicked` method in the `ListFragment` class. If `DetailsFragment` exists (there is a fragment out there with the `DETAILS` tag), it will call the `showDetails` method of `DetailsFragment`:

```
private void onVideoClicked(VideoItem video) {
  DetailFragment detailsFragment = (DetailFragment)
   getFragmentManager().findFragmentByTag(
    MainActivity.TAG_DETAILS_FRAGMENT);
if (detailsFragment != null) {
  detailsFragment.setVideo(video);
 }
}
```

17. We are almost done. In the `activity_main.xml` layout, we created a container for our fragment. Now we will add some code to show the content for `ListFragment` in that container. In the `MainActivity` class, add two private members for both the fragments:

```
private DetailFragment mDetailsFragment;
private ListFragment mListFragment;
```

18. Create `ListFragment` and add it to the container:

```
mListFragment = new ListFragment();
FragmentTransaction ft =
 getFragmentManager().beginTransaction();
ft.add(R.id.main_container_for_list_fragment,
 mListFragment, TAG_LIST_FRAGMENT);
ft.commit();
```

19. Let's create another layout for the main activity but this time it will be one for the large screens, let's say tablets. To the `res` folder, add a new Android resource directory by right-clicking on the `res` item. Choose **layout** for **resource type**, name the directory `layout-large`, and click on the To button.

20. Within the new `layout-large` directory, add a new layout and name it `activity_main` as well. A tablet device is big enough to hold both our fragments so for this layout, we will create two containers: one for the list and one for the details:

```
<?xml version="1.0" encoding="utf-8"?>
<FrameLayout xmlns:android=
 "http://schemas.android.com/apk/res/android"
android:layout_width="match_parent"
android:layout_height="match_parent"
android:id="@+id/main_container">
<FrameLayout
xmlns:android="http://schemas.android.com/apk/res/android"
android:layout_width="300dp"
android:layout_height="match_parent"
android:background="@android:color/holo_orange_light"
```

```
android:id="@+id/main_container_for_list_fragment">
</FrameLayout>
<FrameLayout
android:id="@+id/main_container_for_detail_fragment"
android:background="@android:color/holo_blue_light"
android:layout_marginLeft="300dp"
android:layout_width="match_parent"
android:layout_height="match_parent">
</FrameLayout>
</FrameLayout>
```

21. Modify the `onCreate` implementation for `MainActivity`. If the container is available, we will load the details fragment as well. Move the `commit` call to the end:

```
mListFragment = new ListFragment();
FragmentTransaction ft =
 getFragmentManager().beginTransaction();
ft.add(R.id.main_container_for_list_fragment,
 mListFragment, TAG_LIST_FRAGMENT);
if (findViewById(
 R.id.main_container_for_detail_fragment)!= null){
  mDetailsFragment = new DetailFragment();
  ft.add(R.id.main_container_for_detail_fragment,
  mDetailsFragment, TAG_DETAILS_FRAGMENT);
}
ft.commit();
```

22. One more thing, if you'll allow me to explain. Well, a couple of things actually. If the app is running on a phone, we need to have some kind of navigation from the list fragment view to the details fragment view. Modify the `onVideoClicked` method in the `MainActivity` file so that in case it does not exist yet, the detail fragment will be created there:

```
private void onVideoClicked(VideoItem video) {
  DetailFragment detailsFragment = (DetailFragment)
   getFragmentManager().findFragmentByTag(
    MainActivity.TAG_DETAILS_FRAGMENT);
 if (detailsFragment != null) {
   detailsFragment.setVideo(video);
 }
 else
 {
   FragmentTransaction ft =
   getFragmentManager().beginTransaction();
   detailsFragment = new DetailFragment();
   ft.add(R.id.main_container_for_list_fragment,
    detailsFragment, MainActivity.TAG_DETAILS_FRAGMENT);
```

```
        ft.addToBackStack(MainActivity.TAG_DETAILS_FRAGMENT);
        ft.commit();
        detailsFragment.setVideo(video);
    }
}
```

23. The call to `addToBackStack` that we added in the previous step informs the fragment manager about all fragments being on stack, so we can provide a way of navigation. We need to tell our activity how to behave in case the back button is being pressed: do we want to leave the activity or do we want to pop a fragment from stack? We will override the `onBackPressed` method of the `MainActivity`, just like this:

```
@Override
public void onBackPressed() {
if (getFragmentManager().getBackStackEntryCount()>0){
        getFragmentManager().popBackStack();
    }
else {
this.finish();
    }
}
```

And we are done! We had some work to do but now we have got an app that will work on a phone with navigation and that will display both the fragments if there is sufficient space as is the case with a tablet.

To see the differences, run the app on a smart phone and on a tablet as well. On a phone, it will look similar to the following screenshot. On a tablet (you can use Genymotion for that if you do not have one available) both the list and details are shown in a single view:

There's more...

The next recipe will show how to implement the functionality that allows us to watch the video that we have just found. After all, playing videos is what we want!

Media playback

In the previous recipe, we retrieved search results from YouTube and displayed them in a list and detail fragment. The entries found represent videos, so it would be nice if we were able to play them as well in our app. Let's find a way to do this.

Since we do know the video ID, it is not that difficult to compose a URL for it and load them in a web view; however, Google provides an easier solution for this and offers the YouTube Android Player API for this purpose. It has a couple of limitations but is interesting enough to explore.

Getting ready

To go through this recipe, you need to complete the previous recipe as this one picks up where we left off. While I recommend you to test the app on a physical phone and tablet, you can, of course, use Genymotion as well.

If you are using virtual devices, then Google apps (and the YouTube app on which the API and the player depend) will be missing, and the app will fail for that reason. You need to download and install them on the virtual device first.

How to do it...

Let's see how we can extend the app using the following steps, so it can play back a video for us:

1. Download the YouTube Player API from `https://developers.google.com/youtube/android/player/downloads`.

2. In the downloaded file, find the `YouTubeAndroidPlayerApi.jar` file in the `libs` folder and copy it.

3. Open the project from the previous recipe.

4. Find the `libs` folder within the `app` module and paste the `YouTubeAndroidPlayerApi.jar` file.

5. The dependencies in the `build.gradle` file may have already been prepared to include any files in the `lib` file; however if it is not, add the dependency:

   ```
   compile fileTree(dir: 'libs', include: ['YouTubeAndroidPlayerApi.jar'])
   ```

6. Click on the Sync now link, or in case it does not appear, click on the **Sync project with Gradle files** button on the toolbar.

7. In the `MainActivity` class, add a static tag for the player fragment that we are going to create. Also add the private member for `YouTubePlayerFragment` and a public member to store the YouTube player if the initialization succeeds:

```
public static String TAG_PLAYER_FRAGMENT = "PLAYER";
private YouTubePlayerFragment mPlayerFragment;
public YouTubePlayer mYouTubePlayer = null;
```

8. Open `activity_main.xml` in the `layout-large` directory, change the height of the detail fragment to `300dp`, and add `YouTubePlayerFragment` to it. The preview might complain as it is not aware of how things should be rendered, but that is not really an issue as long as the package is being recognized, which will be the case if you have completed steps 5 and 6 successfully:

```xml
<?xml version="1.0" encoding="utf-8"?>
<FrameLayout
xmlns:android="http://schemas.android.com/apk/res/android"
android:layout_width="match_parent"
android:layout_height="match_parent"
android:id="@+id/main_container">
<FrameLayout
xmlns:android="http://schemas.android.com/apk/res/android"
android:layout_width="300dp"
android:layout_height="match_parent"
android:background="@android:color/holo_orange_light"
android:id="@+id/main_container_for_list_fragment">
</FrameLayout>
<FrameLayout
android:id="@+id/main_container_for_detail_fragment"
android:background="@android:color/holo_blue_light"
android:layout_marginLeft="300dp"
android:layout_width="match_parent"
android:layout_height="300dp">
</FrameLayout>
<fragment
android:name="com.google.android.youtube.player.
YouTubePlayerFragment"
android:id="@+id/main_youtube_player_fragment"
android:layout_marginTop="300dp"
android:layout_marginLeft="300dp"
android:layout_width="match_parent"
android:layout_height="match_parent"
android:layout_weight="3"/>
</FrameLayout>
```

9. In `onCreateView`, just before `ft.commit`, find the container for the player fragment and initialize `YouTuberPlayer`:

```
mPlayerFragment = (YouTubePlayerFragment)
 getFragmentManager().findFragmentById(
   R.id.main_youtube_player_fragment);
if (mPlayerFragment != null) {
   ft.add(mPlayerFragment, TAG_PLAYER_FRAGMENT);
   mPlayerFragment.initialize("Your API key", new
    YouTubePlayer.OnInitializedListener()
   {
    @Override
    public void onInitializationSuccess( YouTubePlayer.Provider
      provider, YouTubePlayer youTubePlayer, boolean isRestored)
    {
      mYouTubePlayer = youTubePlayer;
    }
    @Override
    public void onInitializationFailure(YouTubePlayer.Provider
     provider, YouTubeInitializationResult
      youTubeInitializationResult) {

      Log.d(this.getClass().toString(),
       youTubeInitializationResult.toString());
   });
   }
```

10. In `DetailFragment`, add an on click handler for the Play button in the `onCreateView` method, just before returning the view object:

```
view.findViewById(R.id.detail_button_play).setOnClickListener(
 new View.OnClickListener() {
   @Override
   public void onClick(View v) {
     playVideo();
   }
});
```

11. Create the `playVideo` method in `DetailFragment`. If the player fragment is there (on devices with large screens) and has been initialized, it will play the video; if it is not there (on devices with smaller screens), we will create a player fragment, initialize it, and add it to the stack:

```
private void playVideo(){
if (getActivity() != null &&
 ((MainActivity)getActivity()).mYouTubePlayer != null){
   ((MainActivity)getActivity()
```

```
        ).mYouTubePlayer.cueVideo(mVideo.getId());
    }
    else {
        FragmentTransaction ft =
         getFragmentManager().beginTransaction();

        YouTubePlayerFragment playerFragment = new
        YouTubePlayerFragment();
        ft.add(R.id.main_container_for_list_fragment,
        playerFragment, MainActivity.TAG_DETAILS_FRAGMENT);

        ft.addToBackStack(MainActivity.TAG_PLAYER_FRAGMENT);
        ft.commit();
        playerFragment.initialize("Your API key", new
         YouTubePlayer.OnInitializedListener() {
            @Override
           public void onInitializationSuccess(YouTubePlayer.Provider
             provider, YouTubePlayer youTubePlayer, boolean
             isRestored) {
               if (!isRestored) {
                   youTubePlayer.cueVideo(mVideo.getId());
               }
            }
            @Override
           public void onInitializationFailure(YouTubePlayer.Provider
             provider, YouTubeInitializationResult
              youTubeInitializationResult) {
              Log.d(this.getClass().toString(),
               youTubeInitializationResult.toString());
            }
        });
    }
}
```

And with that, we have added a simple but fully functional implementation to play the selected video.

There's more...

There are many options available to play a video, such as fullscreen or in place, with or without buttons, and so on. Using Chrome Cast, media can also be sent to your TV or as we will see in the final recipe, we can create an app for an Android TV.

TV and media centre

Boring! Again there is nothing to see on the TV! At least not something that seems to be interesting enough. Smart TVs running on Android create a whole new interesting world for developers. Finally, we get the screen size we deserve!

However, it also comes with a different type of audience. Users interact with their phones and tablets to a very large extent. When it comes to watching TV, the focus is much more on consuming.

Well, what is there on the TV? Have a cup of tea and start watching the show. Occasionally, users might be interested in some interaction (a phenomenon that mostly appears as a second screen app since not anyone does own a smart TV already), but most of the time, TV watchers just want to lean back.

Getting ready

This recipe requires Android Studio up and running and the latest SDKs installed. In this recipe, we will provide you a brief introduction to a TV app. In only a few steps, we will create a media centre app. Don't worry, you do not need to have an Android TV. We will create a virtual one.

How to do it...

Let's see what we need to do to develop an Android TV app:

1. Create a new project in Android Studio. Name it `PersonalTeeVee` and click on the Next button.

2. Select the TV option and click on the **Next** button.

3. Choose Android TV Activity and click on Next.

4. Enter `TeeVeeActivity` in the **Activity Name** field and `Personal Tee Vee` in the **Title** field and click on the **Finish** button.

5. Android Studio creates a phone and a TV module for you. Change the configuration to TV. You will see something as shown in the following figure:

6. Check out the `AndroidManifest.xml` file in the tv module. Note the lean back feature requirement (which tells us that this is a TV app with fullscreen experience without any heavy interaction and basically is about consuming content such as watching a video). Also note that we do not require a touch screen. The TV screen is too far away to touch. Besides, nobody likes smears on their TV screens:

```
<uses-feature
android:name="android.hardware.touchscreen"
android:required="false" />
<uses-feature
android:name="android.software.leanback"
android:required="true" />
```

7. To test the TV app, we need to have a virtual TV device. Open the **AVD manager** option from the **Tools | Android** menu.

8. Click on the **Create Virtual Device** button.

9. Select TV from the category list and choose a TV device (1080p or better). Click on the Next button.

10. Pick a system image. I chose, for example, **API level 22 x86**. Click on **Next**.

11. Modify the name of the AVD to whatever you think suits best and click on the **Finish** button. A new virtual TV device will be created for you.

12. Start your TV device by clicking on the play button. If it says that **Google Play Services has stopped**, you may ignore this message for now (although you will need it if you want to play a video).

13. Once the device is booted, run your TV app from Android Studio. By default, it looks like this:

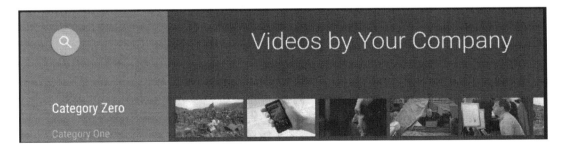

Wow, this is a fully functional media centre app already!

This was just a brief introduction to building an Android TV app. Play with it and tweak it.

There's more...

While the app in this recipe is dedicated to a TV, I see no reason why you couldn't make it an app for any kind of device: phone, phablet, and TV. If you want, you can combine all the recipes in this chapter into a single app. That's a nice challenge, isn't it?

Besides YouTube, there are also interesting media-related APIs to investigate. On `www.programmableweb.com`, for example, you can find some interesting APIs. Some of them are listed here:

API	Navigation
YouTube	http://www.programmableweb.com/api/youtube-live-streaming
Vimeo	http://www.programmableweb.com/api/vimeo
Hey! Spread	http://www.programmableweb.com/api/heyspread
Pirateplay	http://www.programmableweb.com/api/pirateplay
Tinysong	http://www.programmableweb.com/api/tinysong
TwitVid	http://www.programmableweb.com/api/twitvid

Well, now we know where to get media items from, how to play them, and how to automagically create a media centre app.

Coming up next: let's create some media ourselves by capturing some images. See you at the next chapter!

See also

▶   Chapter 6, *Capture and Share*

6

Capture and Share

We love to share the world we live in with others, so we will use our smartphones to take images or videos of all the things and all the people we care about. With Android, this is pretty easy.

In this chapter, you will learn about the following:

- Capturing images the easy way
- Image capturing using the Camera2 API
- Image sharing
- Orientation issues

Introduction

As a developer, you can just launch an intent, grab the data, and do with it whatever you want.

Things become a little bit more complicated if you want to handle image or video capturing yourself. So, why would someone want to do that in the first place? It gives us more flexibility in the way the camera is being previewed, filtered, or handled.

With Android Lollipop onwards, the old Camera API that we had been using has been replaced with the Camera2 API, which has turned out to be a huge improvement. Unfortunately, some orientation issues remain, mostly due to the large fragmentation of Android hardware and software. On some devices, captured images seem to be rotated 90 degrees. Why is that? You will find out in the last recipe in this chapter.

Capturing images the easy way

There are of course, many ways on Android to take a picture or record a video. The easiest way to capture an image is by using an intent to launch the camera app and grabbing the results once the image has been taken.

Getting ready

For this recipe, you just need to have Android Studio up and running.

How to do it...

Launching a camera intent typically goes like this:

1. In Android Studio, create a new project.

2. In the `activity_main.xml` layout, add a new button and an image view. Name the image view `image`.

3. Create an on-click handler for that button.

4. Call the `takePicture` method from the event handler implementation.

5. Implement the `takePicture` method. If supported by the device, launch the capture intent:

```
static final int REQUEST_IMAGE_CAPTURE = 1;
private void takePicture() {
  Intent captureIntent = new
    Intent(MediaStore.ACTION_IMAGE_CAPTURE);

  if (captureIntent.resolveActivity(
    getPackageManager()) != null) {
    startActivityForResult(captureIntent,
      REQUEST_IMAGE_CAPTURE);
  }
}
```

6. Override the `onActivityResult` method. You will get the thumbnail from the data being returned and display the result in the image view:

```
@Override
protected void onActivityResult(int requestCode, int resultCode,
Intent data) {
    if (requestCode == REQUEST_IMAGE_CAPTURE &&
      resultCode == RESULT_OK) {
        Bundle extras = data.getExtras();
        Bitmap thumbBitmap = (Bitmap)
```

```
                    extras.get("data");");
                    ((ImageView)findViewById(R.id.image)
                    ).setImageBitmap(thumbBitmap);
            }
    }
```

This is the easiest way to capture an image, and perhaps you have already done it this way before.

There's more...

If you want to preview the image within your own app, there is more work to do. The Camera2 API can be used for previewing, capturing, and encoding purposes.

Within the Camera2 API, you will find components such as `CameraManager`, `CameraDevice`, `CaptureRequest`, and `CameraCaptureSession`.

Listed here are the most important Camera2 API classes:

Class	Objectives
`CameraManager`	Select camera, create camera device
`CameraDevice`	`Create CaptureRequest,` `CameraCaptureSession`
`CaptureRequest,` `CameraBuilder`	Link to surface view (previewing)
`CameraCaptureSession`	Capture an image and display it on the surface view

The sample that we are going to investigate in the next recipe, *Image capturing*, may look a bit confusing at first. This is mostly because the setup process requires many steps, and most of them will be executed asynchronously. But do not worry, though - we will investigate it step by step.

Image capturing using the Camera2 API

Let us share the world around us with the ones we love. It all starts with previewing and capturing it. That is what this recipe is all about. We will also go back to those good old days when photos were sepia toned.

There are many apps, such as Instagram, that provide options to add filters or effects to your photos. What would happen if sepia were the only option for filtering and sharing your pictures? Maybe we can set a trend. #EverybodyLovesSepia!

We will be using the Camera2 API to capture an image, based on Google's Camera2 Basic sample that is available on GitHub. As a reference for the steps in the recipe, you can have a look at the following class diagram. It will make clear what classes we are dealing with and how they interact with each other:

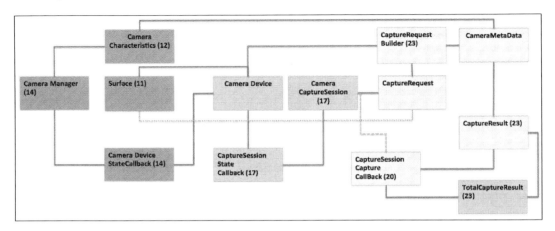

We will investigate what exactly is in there, and once you have found out what is going on, we will add a little bit of ourselves to it by making the preview and the captured image appear in sepia (or another effect, if you prefer).

Getting ready

For this recipe, we will be using the Camera2 API. As we will be using this API, you need to have a real device that is running Android 5.0 or above (recommended), or you will need to create a virtual device.

How to do it...

Let's take a look at how we can get up to speed quickly. Google has already prepared a neat example for us:

1. In Android Studio, choose **Import Android code sample** from the launch wizard, or choose **Import Sample** on the **File** menu.

2. In the next dialog you will see many interesting sample apps demonstrating various Android features. Choose the **Camera2 Basic** sample, and click on the **Next** button:

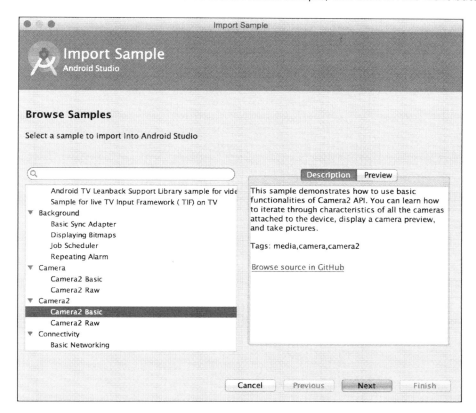

3. Name your project EverybodyLovesSepia and click on the **Finish** button.

If nothing happens after clicking on the button (due to a bug in some versions of Android Studio), try again, but leave the project name unchanged this time.

4. Android Studio will get the sample project from GitHub for you. You can find it at https://github.com/googlesamples/android-Camera2Basic as well.

5. Run the app on a device or on a virtual device.

If you are using a virtual device running on Genymotion, enable the camera first by clicking on the camera icon on the right, turning the camera switch on, and selecting a (web) camera.

Within the app, you will see a preview of the camera, as shown in the following screenshot:

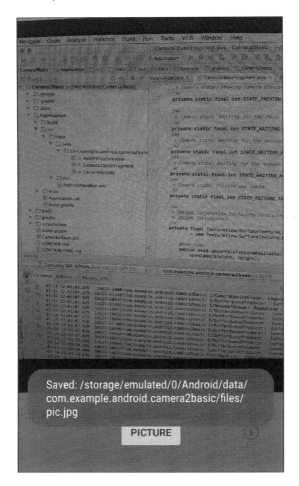

A lot of things have happened automatically again! What is in this Camera2 API sample? What is needed to capture an image? Actually, quite a lot is needed. Open the `Camera2BasicFragment` class. This is where most of the magic happens.

Collapsing all methods

To create a less overwhelming view, collapse all methods:

1. You can do this by choosing the **Folding** option from the **Code** menu. In the submenu, choose **Collapse all**.

2. You will also find other options in this submenu; for example, **Expand all** methods or **Expand** (which expands only the selected method).

Use the shortcuts *Cmd* followed by + and *Cmd* followed by – (or *Ctrl* with + and *Ctrl* with – for Windows) to expand or collapse a method, respectively. Use the shortcuts *Cmd* + *Shift* with + and *Cmd* + *Shift* with – (*Ctrl* + *Shift* and + and *Shift* + *Ctrl* and – for Windows) to expand or collapse, respectively, all methods within a class.

3. Expand the `onViewCreated` method. Here, we see the initialization of `mTextureView`, which is a reference to the custom widget `AutoFitTextureView`. It will display the camera preview.

4. Next, expand the `onResume` method. Initially, this is where the `SurfaceTextureListener` class will be set. As the comments in the sample already suggest, this allows us to wait for the surface to be ready before we try to open a camera. Double click on `mSurfaceTextureListener` and jump to its declaration using the shortcut *Cmd* + *B* (for Windows, that's *Ctrl* + *B*) to see what this is about.

5. Fully expand the initialization of `mSurfaceTextureListener`. Just like an activity, the texture view has a life cycle. Events are being handled here. For now, the most interesting one here is the `onSurfaceTextureAvailable` event. As soon as the surface is available, the `openCamera` method will be called. Double-click on it and jump to it.

6. Many things happen in the `openCamera` method. There is a call to the `setUpCameraOutputs` method. This method will handle which camera to use (if there are multiple ones) by setting the private member `mCameraId` and the (preview) size of the image. This may be different for each type of device. It will also take care of the aspect ratio. Almost any device supports the 4:3 aspect ratio, but many also support 16:9 or other aspect ratios.

Most devices have one or two cameras on board. Some have only a back camera and some have only a front camera. Front cameras often support fewer image sizes and aspect ratios.

Also, with the new permission policy that comes with Android Marshmallow (Android 6.0), your app may not be allowed to use any camera at all. This means that you always need to test whether or not the cameras functionality is available to your app. You will have to provide some feedback to your user by displaying a dialog or toast if it cannot.

7. Next, let's have a look at the following line in the `openCamera` method. It says to open the camera that the `setCameraOutputs` method has selected for us:

```
manager.openCamera(mCameraId, mStateCallback, mBackgroundHandler);
```

8. It also provides a `mStateCallback` parameter. If you double-click on it and jump to it, you can see its declaration. Things are again happening asynchronously here.

9. As soon as the camera has been opened, the preview session will be started. Let's jump to the `createCameraPreviewSession` method.

10. Have a look at `mCameraDevice.createCaptureSession`. One of the parameters that go into that method is a capture session state callback. It is used to determine whether or not the session is configured successfully so the preview can be shown.

11. Now, what needs to be done to take a picture? Find the `onClick` method. You will notice a call to the `takePicture` method. Jump to it. The `takePicture` method in turn calls the `lockFocus` method. Jump to it.

12. Taking a picture involves several steps. The focus of the camera has to be locked. Next, a new capture request needs to be created and the `capture` method needs to be called:

    ```
    mCaptureSession.capture(mPreviewRequestBuilder.build(),
     mCaptureCallback, mBackgroundHandler);
    ```

13. One of the parameters that go into `capture` method is `mCaptureCallback`. Jump to its declaration using *Cmd + B* (or *Ctrl + B* for Windows).

14. You will notice two methods: `onCaptureProgressed` and `onCaptureCompleted`. They both call the private method `process` and pass the result or partial result to it.

15. The `process` method will act differently on the various possible states. Finally, it will call the `captureStillPicture` method. Go to its declaration using *Cmd + B* (or *Ctrl + B* for Windows).

16. The `captureStillPicture` method initializes a `CaptureRequest.Builder` class, which is used to take the picture and store it with the right properties, such as orientation information. Once the capturing is completed and the file has been saved, the camera focus is unlocked and the user is notified through a toast:

    ```
    CameraCaptureSession.CaptureCallback CaptureCallback
       = new CameraCaptureSession.CaptureCallback() {
          @Override
          public void onCaptureCompleted
            (CameraCaptureSession session,
                CaptureRequest request, TotalCaptureResult
                result) {
                  showToast("Saved: " + mFile);
                  unlockFocus();
            }
       };
    ```

The preceding steps showed you the highlights of the basic (!) Camera2 example app. Quite a bit of work for just taking a picture within your app! If you do not need a preview within your app, you may want to consider taking pictures just using an intent. However, having your own preview gives you more flexibility for controls and effects.

Adding the sepia effect

We will add a sepia effect to the preview just because it looks cool (and because of course, everything used to be better in the early days), using the following steps:

1. Go to the `createCameraPreviewSession` method, and within the `onConfigured` class of the camera capture session state call back implementation, add this line just before setting the `autofocus` parameter:

```
mPreviewRequestBuilder.set(
  CaptureRequest.CONTROL_EFFECT_MODE,
    CaptureRequest.CONTROL_EFFECT_MODE_SEPIA);
```

2. If you run your app now, your preview will be in sepia. However, if you press the button to capture an image, it will not have this effect. In the `onCaptureStillPicture` method, you will have to do the same thing. Add this line just above the line that sets the `autofocus` parameter:

```
captureBuilder.set(
  CaptureRequest.CONTROL_EFFECT_MODE,
    CaptureRequest.CONTROL_EFFECT_MODE_SEPIA);
```

Run your app one more time, capture an image, and find the captured file using the Astro app (or another file browser app). You can find it at `Android/data/com.example.android.camera2basic` (Obviously that is if you have accepted the suggested package name or else the path includes the package name you have provided). Sepia it is!

If you like, you can perform some further experiments with the negative or any of the other available effects, which is fun too, at least for a while.

That is it for now. We haven't done much programming yet, but we have looked at some interesting pieces of code. In the next recipe, we will share our captured image on Facebook.

There's more...

For more information, check out GitHub at `https://github.com/googlesamples/android-Camera2Basic` and the Google Camera2 API reference at `https://developer.android.com/reference/android/hardware/camera2/package-summary.html`.

An interesting fork of the Camera2 API sample, with QR code scanning support can be found at `https://github.com/ChristianBecker/Camera2Basic`.

Image sharing

Image capturing is no fun without the ability to share images; for example, on Facebook. We will be using the Facebook SDK for that.

Challenge! If you are building an app running on a Parse backend, as we did in *Chapter 2, Applications with a Cloud-based Backend*, there is no need for that, as the Facebook SDK is already in there. If you want, you can combine the recipes from *Chapter 2, Applications with a Cloud-based Backend* with this one, and create a real cool app real quick!

Getting ready

For this recipe, you need to have the previous recipe completed successfully and you need to have a real Android device (or a virtual one, but this will require some additional steps).

You also need to have a Facebook account, or you can create one just for testing purposes.

How to do it...

Let's take a look at how we can share our sepia captured image on Facebook:

1. Get the code from the previous recipe. Open the `build.gradle` file in the `app` folder. Add a new dependency to the `dependencies` section, and click on the **Sync now** link that will appear after you have added this line:

   ```
   compile 'com.facebook.android:facebook-android-sdk:4.1.0'
   ```

2. To obtain a Facebook app ID, browse to `https://developers.facebook.com` (yeah, this requires a Facebook account). From the **MyApps** menu, choose **Add a new app**, select **Android** as your platform, enter a name for your app, and click on **Create new Facebook App ID**. Choose a category- for example, **Entertainment**- and click on **Create App ID**.

3. Your app will be created, and a QuickStart page will be shown. Scroll down all the way to the **Tell us about your Android project** section. Enter details in the **package name** and **default activity class name** fields, and click on the **Next** button.

4. A pop-up warning will be shown. You can safely ignore the warning and click on the **Use this package name** button. Facebook will start thinking, and after a while the section **Add your development and release key hashes** will appear.

5. To obtain development key hashes, open the Terminal app (in Windows, start Command Prompt) and type the following:

   ```
   keytool -exportcert -alias androiddebugkey -keystore ~/.android/
   debug.keystore | openssl sha1 -binary | openssl base64
   ```

If prompted for the keystore password, enter `android`, which should do the trick - unless you have changed the password previously, of course.

6. Hit *Enter*, copy the value that is shown, and paste it into the Facebook web page at **Development Key Hashes**. Click on the **Next** button to proceed.

7. In the section **Next Steps**, click on the **Skip to developer dashboard** button. It will bring you straight to the information you need, the app ID. Copy the value in the **App ID** field:

8. Next, initialize the Facebook SDK. Open the `CameraActivity` class, and within the `onCreate` method, add the following line just after the `super.OnCreate` line. Use the *Alt + Enter* shortcut to import the required package `com.facebook.FacebookSdk`:

```
FacebookSdk.sdkInitialize(getApplicationContext());
```

9. Now we need to tell the app about the Facebook app ID. Open the `strings.xml` file from the `res/values` folder. Add a new string that will contain your Facebook app id:

```
<string name="facebook_app_id">Your facebook app id</string>
```

10. Open the `AndroidManifest.xml` file.

11. Add a metadata element to the `application` element:

```
<meta-data android:name="com.facebook.sdk.ApplicationId"
android:value="@string/facebook_app_id"/>
```

12. Add a `FacebookActivity` declaration to the `manifest` file:

```
<activity android:name="com.facebook.FacebookActivity"
 android:configChanges=
  "keyboard|keyboardHidden|screenLayout|
   screenSize|orientation"
 android:theme="@android:style/Theme.Translucent.
  NoTitleBar"
 android:label="@string/app_name" />
```

13. In the `Camera2BasicFragment` class, locate the `captureStillPicture` method. Add a new call to the end of the `onCaptureCompleted` callback implementation, just after the `unlockFocus` class:

```
sharePictureOnFacebook();
```

14. Finally, add a provider to the `manifest` file (within the `application` section), which will allow you to share images on Facebook. The next chapter will discuss content providers. For now just append your app ID to the end of `FaceBookContentProvider` at `authorities`, replacing the zeros in the example shown here:

```
<provider android:authorities="com.facebook.app.
  FacebookContentProvider000000000000"
    android:name="com.facebook.FacebookContentProvider"
     android:exported="true" />
```

15. Implement the `sharePictureOnFacebook` method. We will load the bitmap from the file. In a real app, we would have to calculate the required value for `inSampleSize`, but for the sake of simplicity, we will just use a fixed `inSampleSize` setting of 4 here. On most devices, this will be sufficient to avoid any `OutOfMemory` exceptions that may occur otherwise. Also, we will add the photo to the `share` dialog that will be displayed after taking a picture:

```
private void sharePictureOnFacebook(){
    final BitmapFactory.Options options = new
     BitmapFactory.Options();
    options.inJustDecodeBounds = false;
    options.inSampleSize = 4;
    Bitmap bitmap =
     BitmapFactory.decodeFile(mFile.getPath(), options);
    SharePhoto photo = new
    SharePhoto.Builder().setBitmap(bitmap).build();
    SharePhotoContent content = new
    SharePhotoContent.Builder().addPhoto(photo).build();
    ShareDialog.show(getActivity(), content);
}
```

16. To be on the safe side, we want to create a unique file name for each picture. Modify the `onActivityCreated` method to do so:

```
@Override
public void onActivityCreated(Bundle savedInstanceState) {
    super.onActivityCreated(savedInstanceState);
    mFile = new
    File(getActivity().getExternalFilesDir(null),
      "pic"+ new Date().getTime()+".jpg");
}
```

17. The page will look like this on your Facebook timeline. Here it is shown in the Dutch language:

18. Run the app and share some sepia images on your own Facebook timeline!

Our app is fully functional already, although it may require a few tweaks. On my Samsung device, all images that I have captured in portrait mode are rotated 90 degrees. That is just a little bit too artistic. Let's fix it in the next recipe!

Orientation issues

On some devices (such as the Samsung ones), captured images in portrait mode are rotated 90 degrees; and on other devices (such as the Nexus devices), things seem to be just fine. You won't notice this if you have a look at the file using the Astro app, for example, but you will if you see the preview in the Facebook **share** dialog.

This is a well-known challenge for many Android developers. Images may contain metadata about the rotation degree, but apparently not every app respects that metadata. What is the best solution? Should you rotate the image every time you want to display it? Should you rotate the bitmap itself, which could be very time and processor consuming?

Getting ready

For this recipe, you need to have the previous recipe completed successfully. It would be ideal if you had multiple Android devices to test your app on. Otherwise, it would be great if you had at least a Samsung device available, as the orientation issue can be reproduced for most (if not all) models from this brand.

How to do it...

Let's take a look at how you can fix this orientation issue if it appears:

1. In the Facebook **share** dialog, the preview image is rotated 90 degrees (on some devices), as shown here:

2. This does not look like the world I live in. It appears this way on my Samsung Galaxy Note 3 device, but not on my Nexus 5 device. Apparently, Samsung stores the picture as it is from a landscape point of view, and then adds metadata to it to indicate that the image has been rotated (compared to the default orientation). Things, however, will go wrong if you want to share it on Facebook, for example, as the orientation information in the metadata is not being respected.

3. So, we need to examine the meta data and find out if there is any rotation information in there. Add the `getRotationFromMetaData` method:

```
private int getRotationFromMetaData(){
    try {
        ExifInterface exif = new
        ExifInterface(mFile.getAbsolutePath());

        int orientation = exif.getAttributeInt(
         ExifInterface.TAG_ORIENTATION,
          ExifInterface.ORIENTATION_NORMAL);
        switch (orientation) {
            case ExifInterface.ORIENTATION_ROTATE_270:
                return 270;
            case ExifInterface.ORIENTATION_ROTATE_180:
                return 180;
            case ExifInterface.ORIENTATION_ROTATE_90:
                return 90;
            default:
                return 0;
        }
    }
    catch (IOException ex){
        return 0;
    }
}
```

4. If needed, you have to rotate the bitmap before showing the sharing preview. That is where the `rotateCaptureImageIfNeeded` method comes in.

    Here, we can safely rotate the bitmap in memory, because of the `inSampleSet` value of `4`. If you rotate the original full-size bitmap, chances are that you will run out of memory. Either way, it is going to be time consuming and will result in a delay between capturing an image and displaying the sharing preview dialog:

```
private Bitmap rotateCapturedImageIfNeeded(Bitmap bitmap){
    int rotate = getRotationFromMetaData();
    Matrix matrix = new Matrix();
    matrix.postRotate(rotate);
    bitmap = Bitmap.createBitmap(bitmap, 0, 0, bitmap.getWidth(),
     bitmap.getHeight(), matrix, true);
```

```
    Bitmap mutableBitmap = bitmap.copy(Bitmap.Config.ARGB_8888,
     true);
   return mutableBitmap;
}
```

5. Then, in the `sharePictureOnFacebook` method, right after you have retrieved the bitmap using the `BitmapFactory` class , call the `onRotateCaptureImageIfNeeded` method and pass the bitmap as a parameter:

   ```
   bitmap = rotateCapturedImageIfNeeded(bitmap);
   ```

6. If you run the app again, you will see that everything is fine in portrait mode too:

These things are easy to implement and will improve the quality of your app, although they can also drive you nuts sometimes and make you wonder why one solution cannot just work on any device. Everything looks fine now, but what will it look like on a tablet or on a Huawei, LG, or HTC device? There's nothing that cannot be fixed, but since you do not have a drawerful of Android devices (or maybe you do), testing is hard.

It always is a good thing to test your app on as many devices as possible. Consider using a service for remote testing, for example, TestDroid. You can find their website at www.testdroid.com. In *Chapter 8, Improving quality*, this and other topics will be discussed, but first will we have a look at observables and content providers in the upcoming chapter.

There's more...

Capturing video is even more fun to do. There is also a Camera2 API sample for video capturing available. You can examine the sample project through the **Import sample** option as well.

See also

▶ *Chapter 8, Improving quality*

7

Content Providers and Observers

In most apps, we need to persist data and often use SQLite for this purpose.

A very common situation is that of the list and detail views. By using content providers, we do not just provide a way of communication between apps but also save ourselves much work in our own app.

In this chapter, you will learn about:

▸ Content providers

▸ Consuming and updating data using a content provider

▸ Changing projections to display **Key Performance Indicators** (**KPIs**) in your app

▸ Communicating with other apps using content providers

Introduction

If we want to create a new row or if we want to edit a row in the database, the app will show the fragment or activity containing the details, where the user can enter or modify some text and other values. Once the record has been inserted or updated, the list needs to know about the changes. Telling the list activity or fragment about the changes is not hard to do, but there is a more elegant way to accomplish this. For this, and for other reasons that we will find out about later, we will examine what content providers are about.

The Android content provider framework allows us to create a much better design for our app. One of its features is that it allows us to notice when certain data has been changed. That could work even across different applications.

Content providers

Building a content provider is a really smart thing to do. The content provider API comes with an interesting feature that allows applications to observe changes in a data set.

Content providers connect data in one process with code running in another process, even between two completely different applications if you want. If you ever wrote code to pick an image from the Gallery app, you may have experienced this behavior. Some component manipulates the persistent dataset that other components depend upon. A content provider can use many different ways to store data, which can be stored in a database, in files, or even over a network.

Datasets are identified by unique URIs, so it is possible to ask for notifications if a certain URI is changed. Here is where the observer pattern comes in.

The observer pattern is a common software design pattern in which an object (the subject) has one or more dependents (the observers, also known as the listeners) that will automatically be notified of any state changes.

There's more...

Design patterns

To learn more about this and other **object-oriented** (**OO**) design patterns, you can have a look at http://www.oodesign.com/observer-pattern.html.

RxJava

RxJava is a very interesting library and is available in an Android flavor as well. Reactive programming has principal similarities with the observer pattern. The basic building blocks of reactive code are also Observables and Subscribers.

To learn more about Rx and RxJava, you can visit these web sites:

- https://github.com/reactivex/rxandroid
- https://github.com/ReactiveX/RxJava/wiki/How-To-Use-RxJava
- http://blog.danlew.net/2014/09/15/grokking-rxjava-part-1/

See also

- *Chapter 8*, *Improving Quality*

Consuming and updating data using a content provider – daily thoughts

To demonstrate how to create and use content providers we will create an app to store what is on your mind and how happy you are on a daily basis.

Yes, there are apps doing that; however, if you want to create an app to record sport notes and scores instead, feel free to modify the code as it involves basically the same functionality.

In this recipe, we will store new thoughts and retrieve them using a content provider. For the various elements of the app, we will be using fragments because they will neatly demonstrate the effect of the observer pattern.

Getting ready

For this recipe, you just need to have Android Studio up and running and a physical or virtual Android device.

How to do it...

Let's see how to set up a project using a content provider. We will be using the Navigation Drawer template for it:

1. Create a new project in Android Studio and name it `DailyThoughts`. Click on the **Next** button.
2. Select the **Phone and Tablet** option and click on the **Next** button.
3. Choose **Navigation Drawer Activity** and click on the **Next** button.
4. Accept all values on the **Customize the Activity** page and click on the **Finish** button.
5. Open the `strings.xml` file within the `res/values` folder. Modify the strings for the entries that start with `title_section`. Replace them with the menu items needed for our app. Also replace the `action_sample` string:

   ```
   <string name="title_section_daily_notes">Daily
     thoughts</string>
   <string name="title_section_note_list">Thoughts
     list</string>
   <string name="action_add">Add thought</string>
   ```

6. Open the `NavigationDrawerFragment` file, and in the `onCreate` method, modify the strings for the adapter accordingly:

```
mDrawerListView.setAdapter(new ArrayAdapter<String>(
        getActionBar().getThemedContext(),
        android.R.layout.simple_list_item_activated_1,
        android.R.id.text1,
        new String[]{
                getString(R.string.title_section_daily_notes),
                getString(R.string.title_section_note_list)
        }));
```

7. In the same class, within the `onOptionsItemSelected` method, remove the second `if` statement that is displaying a toast. We do not need it.

8. Open `main.xml` from the `res/menu` folder. Remove the item for the settings and modify the first item so it will use the `action_add` string. Also rename it's ID and add a neat icon for it:

```
<menu xmlns:android=
  "http://schemas.android.com/apk/res/android"
  xmlns:tools="http://schemas.android.com/tools"
    tools:context=".MainActivity">
<item android:id="@+id/action_add"
  android:title="@string/action_add"
    android:icon="@android:drawable/ic_input_add"
      android:showAsAction="withText|ifRoom" />
</menu>
```

9. In the `MainActivity` file, in the `onSectionAttached` section, apply the correct strings for the different options:

```
public void onSectionAttached(int number) {
    switch (number) {
        case 0:
            mTitle = getString(
              R.string.title_section_daily_notes);
            break;
        case 1:
            mTitle = getString(
              R.string.title_section_note_list);
            break;
    }
}
```

10. Create a new package named db. Within this package, create a new class, DatabaseHelper, that extends the SQLiteOpenHelper class. It will help us to create a new database for our application. It will contain just one table: thoughts. Each Thought table will have an id, a name and a happiness rating:

```
public class DatabaseHelper extends SQLiteOpenHelper {
    public static final String DATABASE_NAME =
      "DAILY_THOUGHTS";
    public static final String THOUGHTS_TABLE_NAME =
      "thoughts";
    static final int DATABASE_VERSION = 1;
    static final String CREATE_DB_TABLE =
      " CREATE TABLE " + THOUGHTS_TABLE_NAME +
      " (_id INTEGER PRIMARY KEY AUTOINCREMENT, " +
      " name TEXT NOT NULL, " +
      " happiness INT NOT NULL);";
    public DatabaseHelper(Context context){
        super(context, DATABASE_NAME, null,
          DATABASE_VERSION);
    }
    @Override
    public void onCreate(SQLiteDatabase db)
    {
        db.execSQL(CREATE_DB_TABLE);
    }
    @Override
    public void onUpgrade(SQLiteDatabase db, int
      oldVersion, int newVersion) {
        db.execSQL("DROP TABLE IF EXISTS " +
          THOUGHTS_TABLE_NAME);
        onCreate(db);
    }
}
```

11. Create another package and name it providers. Within this package, create a new class called ThoughtsProvider. This will be our content provider for all our daily thoughts. Make it a descendant of the ContentProvider class.

12. From the **Code** menu, choose the **Implement methods** option. In the dialog that appears, all available methods are selected. Accept this suggestion and click on the **OK** button. Your new class will be extended with these methods.

13. On top of the class, we will create some static variables:

```
static final String PROVIDER_NAME =
  "com.packt.dailythoughts";
static final String URL = "content://" + PROVIDER_NAME +
  "/thoughts";
```

```
public static final Uri CONTENT_URI = Uri.parse(URL);
public static final String THOUGHTS_ID = "_id";
public static final String THOUGHTS_NAME = "name";
public static final String THOUGHTS_HAPPINESS =
  "happiness";
static final int THOUGHTS = 1;
static final int THOUGHT_ID = 2;
static final UriMatcher uriMatcher;
static{
    uriMatcher = new UriMatcher(UriMatcher.NO_MATCH);
    uriMatcher.addURI(PROVIDER_NAME, "thoughts",
     THOUGHTS);
    uriMatcher.addURI(PROVIDER_NAME, "thoughts/#",
     THOUGHT_ID);
}
```

14. Add a private member, db, that refers to the SQLiteDatabase class, and modify the onCreate method. We create a new database helper:

```
private SQLiteDatabase db;
@Override
public boolean onCreate() {
    Context context = getContext();
    DatabaseHelper dbHelper = new DatabaseHelper(context);
    db = dbHelper.getWritableDatabase();
    return (db == null)? false:true;
}
```

Queries

Next, implement the query method. A query returns a cursor object. A cursor represents the result of the query and points to one of the query results so the results can be buffered efficiently as it does not need to load data into memory:

```
private static HashMap<String, String>
  THOUGHTS_PROJECTION;
@Override
public Cursor query(Uri uri, String[] projection,
  String selection, String[] selectionArgs, String
   sortOrder) {
    SQLiteQueryBuilder builder = new
    SQLiteQueryBuilder();
    builder.setTables(
     DatabaseHelper.THOUGHTS_TABLE_NAME);
    switch (uriMatcher.match(uri)) {
       case THOUGHTS:
         builder.setProjectionMap(
          THOUGHTS_PROJECTION);
         break;
```

```
  case THOUGHT_ID:
    builder.appendWhere( THOUGHTS_ID + "=" +
     uri.getPathSegments().get(1));
    break;
  default:
    throw new IllegalArgumentException(
      "Unknown URI: " + uri);
}
if (sortOrder == null || sortOrder == ""){
    sortOrder = THOUGHTS_NAME;
}
Cursor c = builder.query(db, projection,
 selection, selectionArgs,null, null, sortOrder);
c.setNotificationUri(
 getContext().getContentResolver(), uri);
return c;
}
```

 The setNotificationUri call registers the instruction to watch a content URI for changes.

We will implement the other methods using the following steps:

1. Implement the getType method. The dir directory suggests we want to get all thought records. The item term indicates that we are looking for a particular thought:

```
@Override
public String getType(Uri uri) {
    switch (uriMatcher.match(uri)){
      case THOUGHTS:
        return "vnd.android.cursor.dir/vnd.df.thoughts";
      case THOUGHT_ID:
        return "vnd.android.cursor.item/vnd.df.thoughts";
      default:
        throw new IllegalArgumentException(
          "Unsupported URI: " + uri);
    }
}
```

2. Implement the insert method. It will create a new record based on the provided values, and if this succeeds we will be notified about the change:

```
@Override
public Uri insert(Uri uri, ContentValues values) {
    long rowID = db.insert(
     DatabaseHelper.THOUGHTS_TABLE_NAME , "", values);
```

```
        if (rowID > 0)
        {
          Uri _uri = ContentUris.withAppendedId(CONTENT_URI,
            rowID);
          getContext().getContentResolver().notifyChange( _uri,
            null);
          return _uri;
        }
        throw new SQLException("Failed to add record: " +
          uri);
}
```

3. The `delete` and `update` methods are out of scope for this recipe, so we will not implement them now. Challenge: Add your own implementation here.

4. Open the `AndroidManifest.xml` file and add add the `provider` tag within the `application` tag:

```
<provider
    android:name=".providers.ThoughtsProvider"
    android:authorities="com.packt.dailythoughts"
    android:readPermission=
      "com.packt.dailythoughts.READ_DATABASE"
    android:exported="true" />
```

> For security reasons, you should use `false` as the value for the exported property in most cases. The reason why we set the value of this property to `true` here is that later we will create another app that will be able to read the content from this app.

5. Add the permission for other apps to read data. We will use that in the last recipe. Add it outside the `application` tag:

```
<permission
  android:name="com.packt.dailythoughts.READ_DATABASE"
    android:protectionLevel="normal"/>
```

6. Open the `strings.xml` file and add new strings to it:

```
<string name="my_thoughts">My thoughts</string>
<string name="save">Save</string>
<string name="average_happiness">Average
  happiness</string>
```

7. Create two new layout files: `fragment_thoughts.xml` for our list of thoughts and `fragment_thoughts_detail` to enter new thoughts.

8. Define the layout for `fragment_thoughts.xml`. A `ListView` widget is just fine to display all thoughts:

```xml
<?xml version="1.0" encoding="utf-8"?>
<LinearLayout xmlns:android=
  "http://schemas.android.com/apk/res/android"
    android:layout_width="match_parent"
     android:layout_height="match_parent"
     android:orientation="vertical" >
    <ListView
        android:id="@+id/thoughts_list"
        android:layout_width="match_parent"
        android:layout_height="wrap_content" >
    </ListView>
</LinearLayout>
```

9. The layout for `fragment_thoughts_detail.xml` will contain the `EditText` and `RatingBar` widgets so we can enter what we are thinking and how happy how we currently are:

```xml
<?xml version="1.0" encoding="utf-8"?>
<LinearLayout xmlns:android=
  "http://schemas.android.com/apk/res/android"
    android:orientation="vertical"
    android:layout_gravity="center"
    android:layout_margin="32dp"
    android:padding="16dp"
    android:layout_width="match_parent"
    android:background=
      "@android:color/holo_green_light"
    android:layout_height="wrap_content">
    <TextView
        android:layout_margin="8dp"
        android:textSize="16sp"
        android:text="@string/my_thoughts"
      android:layout_width="match_parent"
    android:layout_height="wrap_content" />
    <EditText
        android:id="@+id/thoughts_edit_thoughts"
        android:layout_margin="8dp"
        android:layout_width="match_parent"
        android:layout_height="wrap_content" />
    <RatingBar
        android:id="@+id/thoughs_rating_bar_happy"
        android:layout_width="wrap_content"
        android:layout_height="wrap_content"
        android:layout_gravity="center_horizontal"
        android:clickable="true"
        android:numStars="5"
        android:rating="0" />
```

```
        <Button
            android:id="@+id/thoughts_detail_button"
            android:text="@string/save"
            android:layout_width="match_parent"
            android:layout_height="wrap_content" />
    </LinearLayout>
```

10. Also create a layout for the rows in the list of thoughts. Name it `adapter_thought.xml`. Add text views to display an ID a title, or name and the rating:

```
<?xml version="1.0" encoding="utf-8"?>
<LinearLayout xmlns:android=
  "http://schemas.android.com/apk/res/android"
    android:orientation="vertical"
    android:layout_width="match_parent"
    android:padding="8dp"
    android:layout_height="match_parent">
    <TextView
        android:textSize="32sp"
        android:text="0"
        android:textStyle="bold"
        android:layout_width="match_parent"
        android:layout_height="wrap_content"
        android:id="@+id/adapter_thought_id"/>
    <TextView
        android:id="@+id/adapter_thought_title"
        android:textSize="18sp"
        android:maxLines="2"
        android:ellipsize="end"
        android:layout_margin="4dp"
        android:layout_width="match_parent"
        android:layout_height="wrap_content" />
    <TextView
        android:id="@+id/adapter_thought_rating"
        android:textSize="24sp"
        android:textStyle="bold"
        android:textColor=
          "@android:color/holo_green_dark"
        android:layout_width="match_parent"
        android:layout_height="wrap_content" />
</LinearLayout>
```

11. Create a new package, name it: `fragments`, and add two new classes to it: `ThoughtsDetailFragment` and `ThoughtsFragment`, both of which will be descendants of the `Fragment` class.

12. To the `ThoughtsFragment` class, add the `LoaderCallBack` implementation:

```
public class ThoughtsFragment extends Fragment
   implements
     LoaderManager.LoaderCallbacks<Cursor>{
```

13. From the **Code** menu, choose **Implement methods**, accept the suggested methods, and click on the **OK** button. It will create the `onCreateLoader`, `onLoadFinished`, and `onLoaderReset` implementations.

14. Add two private members that will hold the list view and an adapter:

```
private ListView mListView;
private SimpleCursorAdapter mAdapter;
```

15. Override the `onCreateView` method, where we will inflate the layout and get a reference to the list view. From here we also will call the `getData` method:

```
@Override
public View onCreateView(LayoutInflater inflater, ViewGroup
container, Bundle savedInstanceState) {
    final View view = inflater.inflate(
     R.layout.fragment_thoughts, container, false);
    mListView = (ListView)view.findViewById(
     R.id.thoughts_list);
    getData();
    return view;
}
```

Loader manager

The following steps will help us to add a loader manager to our app:

1. Implement the `getData` method. We will use the `initLoader` method of `loaderManager` for that. The projection defines the fields we want to retrieve, and the target is an array of ID's within the `adapter_thought_title` layout, which will save us some work using the `SimpleCursorAdapter` class.

```
private void getData(){
    String[] projection = new String[] {
     ThoughtsProvider.THOUGHTS_ID,
     ThoughtsProvider.THOUGHTS_NAME,
     ThoughtsProvider.THOUGHTS_HAPPINESS};
    int[] target = new int[] {
     R.id.adapter_thought_id,
     R.id.adapter_thought_title,
     R.id.adapter_thought_rating };

    getLoaderManager().initLoader(0, null, this);

    mAdapter = new SimpleCursorAdapter(getActivity(),
```

```
        R.layout.adapter_thought, null, projection,
          target, 0);
       mListView.setAdapter(mAdapter);
}
```

2. After the `initLoader` call, a new loader needs to be created. For this we will have to implement the `onLoadFinished` method. We use the same projection as we did for the adapter and we will create a `CursorLoader` class using the `uri` content of the `ThoughtsProvider` we have created in the preceding steps. We will sort the outcome by ID (descending):

```
@Override
public Loader<Cursor> onCreateLoader(int id, Bundle args) {
        String[] projection = new String[] {
      ThoughtsProvider.THOUGHTS_ID,
      ThoughtsProvider.THOUGHTS_NAME,
      ThoughtsProvider.THOUGHTS_HAPPINESS};
      String sortBy = "_id DESC";
      CursorLoader cursorLoader = new
      CursorLoader(getActivity(),
      ThoughtsProvider.CONTENT_URI, projection, null,
       null, sortBy);
      return cursorLoader;
}
```

3. In `onLoadFinished`, notify the adapter about the loaded data:

```
mAdapter.swapCursor(data);
```

4. Finally, let's add the implementation for the `onLoaderReset` method. In this situation, the data is no longer available so we can delete the reference.

```
mAdapter.swapCursor(null);
```

5. Let's have a look at the `ThoughtsDetailFragment` method. Override the `onCreateView` method, inflate the layout, and add an on-click listener for the save button in the layout:

```
@Override
public View onCreateView(LayoutInflater inflater, ViewGroup
container, Bundle savedInstanceState) {
    final View view = inflater.inflate(
      R.layout.fragment_thoughts_detail, container,
        false);
    view.findViewById(
      R.id.thoughts_detail_button).setOnClickListener(
```

```
    new View.OnClickListener() {
        @Override
        public void onClick(View v) {
            addThought();
        }
    });
    return view;
}
```

6. Add the `addThought` method. We will create new content values based on the input via the `EditText` and `RatingBar` field We will use the `insert` method of the content resolver based on the provided URI. After inserting the new record, we will clear the input:

```
private void addThought(){
    EditText thoughtsEdit =
      (EditText)getView().findViewById(
       R.id.thoughts_edit_thoughts);
    RatingBar happinessRatingBar =
      (RatingBar)getView().findViewById(
       R.id.thoughs_rating_bar_happy);
    ContentValues values = new ContentValues();
    values.put(ThoughtsProvider.THOUGHTS_NAME,
      thoughtsEdit.getText().toString());
    values.put(ThoughtsProvider.THOUGHTS_HAPPINESS,
      happinessRatingBar.getRating());
    getActivity().getContentResolver().insert(
      ThoughtsProvider.CONTENT_URI, values);
    thoughtsEdit.setText("");
    happinessRatingBar.setRating(0);
}
```

7. Again it is time to glue things together. Open the `MainActivity` class and add two private members that will refer to the fragments we have created as follows:

```
private ThoughtsFragment mThoughtsFragment;
private ThoughtsDetailFragment mThoughtsDetailFragment;
```

8. Add two private members that will initialize them if needed, and return the instance:

```
private ThoughtsFragment getThoughtsFragment(){
    if (mThoughtsFragment==null) {
        mThoughtsFragment = new ThoughtsFragment();
    }
    return mThoughtsFragment;
}
private ThoughtsDetailFragment
getThoughtDetailFragment() {
```

```
        if (mThoughtsDetailFragment==null){
         mThoughtsDetailFragment = new
            ThoughtsDetailFragment();
         }
         return mThoughtsDetailFragment;
      }
```

9. Remove the implementation for `onNavigationDrawerItemSelected` and a new one to display the list of thoughts. We will implement the KPI option later:

```
@Override
public void onNavigationDrawerItemSelected(int
   position) {
   FragmentManager fragmentManager =
     getFragmentManager();
   if (position==1) {
         fragmentManager.beginTransaction().
          replace(R.id.container,
            getThoughtsFragment()).commit();
   }
}
```

10. In the `onOptionsItemSelected` method, test whether the id is `action_add`, and if so, display the details fragment. Add the implementation just after the line where we get the id:

```
if (id== R.id.action_add)
{
    FragmentManager fragmentManager =
     getFragmentManager();
    fragmentManager.beginTransaction().add(
     R.id.container, getThoughtDetailFragment()
       ).commit();
}
```

 Instead of `replace`, we use `add` here. We want the details fragment to appear on top of the stack.

11. After saving details, the fragment has to be removed again. Open `ThoughtsDetailFragment` one more time. To the end of the `addThought` method, add this to do the trick:

```
getActivity().getFragmentManager().beginTransaction().
  remove(this).commit();
```

12. However, it would be better to let the activity handle the displaying of fragments since they are intended to be helpers to an activity. Instead, we will create a listener for an `onSave` event. On top of the class, add a `DetailFragmentListener` interface. Also create a private member and a setter for it:

```
public interface DetailFragmentListener {
    void onSave();
}
private DetailFragmentListener
 mDetailFragmentListener;
public void setDetailFragmentListener(
 DetailFragmentListener listener){
    mDetailFragmentListener = listener;
}
```

13. Add these lines to the end of the `addThought` member to let the listener know things have been saved:

```
if (mDetailFragmentListener != null){
    mDetailFragmentListener.onSave();
}
```

14. Go back to the `MainActivity` class, and add a listener implementation for it. You could use the **Implement methods** option from the **Code** menu for it if you want:

```
public class MainActivity extends Activity
   implements NavigationDrawerFragment.
    NavigationDrawerCallbacks,
     ThoughtsDetailFragment.DetailFragmentListener {
@Override
public void onSave() {
  getFragmentManager().beginTransaction().remove(
    mThoughtsDetailFragment).commit();
}
```

15. To tell the detail fragment that the main activity is listening, scroll to the `getThoughtDetailFragment` class and call the `setListener` method right after the creation of a new detail fragment:

```
mThoughtsDetailFragment.setDetailFragmentListener(this);
```

Now run the app, choose **Thoughts list** from the navigation drawer, and click on the plus sign to add new thoughts. Following screenshot gives the example of adding thought:

We do not need to tell the fragment that contains the list about the new thought we have created in the detail fragment. Using a content provider with an observer, the list will be updated automatically.

This way we can accomplish more and achieve less error-prone functionality writing less code, which is exactly what we want. It allows us to improve the quality of our code.

See also

► Refer *Chapter 5, Size Does Matter*
► Refer *Chapter 8, Improving Quality*

Change projections to display KPIs in your app

We can use a different projection and the same observer pattern for displaying some KPIs. Actually that is pretty easy, as we will see in this recipe.

Getting ready

For this recipe, you need to have completed the previous one successfully.

How to do it...

We will continue working on the app from the previous recipe and we will add a new view to display the KPIs:

1. Open the project you have worked on in the previous recipe.

2. Add a new layout, `fragment_thoughts_kpi.xml`:

```xml
<?xml version="1.0" encoding="utf-8"?>
<LinearLayout xmlns:android=
  "http://schemas.android.com/apk/res/android"
  android:orientation="vertical"
  android:layout_width="match_parent"
  android:gravity="center_horizontal"
  android:padding="16dp"
  android:layout_height="match_parent">
  <TextView
        android:id="@+id/thoughts_kpi_count"
        android:textSize="32sp"
        android:layout_margin="16dp"
        android:layout_width="wrap_content"
        android:layout_height="wrap_content" />
    <TextView
        android:id="@+id/thoughts_kpi_avg_happiness"
        android:text= "@string/average_happiness"
        android:textSize="32sp"
        android:layout_margin="16dp"
        android:layout_width="wrap_content"
        android:layout_height="wrap_content" />
```

```xml
        <RatingBar
            android:id="@+id/thoughts_rating_bar_happy"
            android:layout_width="wrap_content"
            android:layout_height="wrap_content"
            android:layout_gravity="center_horizontal"
            android:clickable="false"
            android:numStars="5"
            android:rating="0" />
    </LinearLayout>
```

3. Add a new fragment and name it `ThoughtsKpiFragment`. It descends from the `Fragment` class. We will be using the `LoaderManager` here as well so it will basically look like this:

```java
public class ThoughtsKpiFragment extends Fragment
  implements LoaderManager.LoaderCallbacks<Cursor> {
    @Override
    public Loader<Cursor> onCreateLoader(int id, Bundle args) {
        return null;
    }
    @Override
    public void onLoadFinished(Loader<Cursor> loader, Cursor
     data) {
    }
    @Override
    public void onLoaderReset(Loader<Cursor> loader) {
    }
}
```

4. Because we will be using two loaders to display two different KPIs, we are going to add two constant values first:

```java
public static int LOADER_COUNT_THOUGHTS = 1;
public static int LOADER_AVG_RATING = 2;
```

5. Override the `onCreate` method:

```java
@Override
public View onCreateView(LayoutInflater inflater, ViewGroup
container, Bundle savedInstanceState) {
    final View view = inflater.inflate(
     R.layout.fragment_thoughts_kpi, container, false);
    getKpis();
    return view;
}
```

6. Create the `getKpis` method (where we initialize the loader twice for different purposes):

```
private void getKpis(){
    getLoaderManager().initLoader(LOADER_COUNT_THOUGHTS, null,
      this);
    getLoaderManager().initLoader(LOADER_AVG_RATING, null,
      this);
}
```

7. Add the implementation for the `onCreateLoader` method. This time the projection depends on the id of the loader. The projection is just like you would expect it to be if it was plain SQL. We are counting the number of rows and we are calculating the average happiness:

```
@Override
public Loader<Cursor> onCreateLoader(int id, Bundle args) {
    if (id == LOADER_COUNT_THOUGHTS) {
      String[] projection = new String[] {"COUNT(*) AS kpi"};
      android.content.CursorLoader cursorLoader = new
      android.content.CursorLoader(getActivity(),
        ThoughtsProvider.CONTENT_URI, projection, null, null,
          null);
      return cursorLoader;
    }
    else {
      String[] projection = new String[]
        {"AVG(happiness) AS kpi"};
      android.content.CursorLoader cursorLoader = new
      android.content.CursorLoader(getActivity(),
       ThoughtsProvider.CONTENT_URI, projection, null, null,
         null);
      return cursorLoader;
    }
}
```

8. Once the data comes in, we arrive at the `onLoadFinished` method and will call methods to display the data, if there is any:

```
@Override
public void onLoadFinished(Loader<Cursor> loader, Cursor data) {
    if (data == null || !data.moveToNext()) {
        return;
    }
    if (loader.getId() == LOADER_COUNT_THOUGHTS) {
        setCountedThoughts(data.getInt(0));
    }
```

```
        else{
            setAvgHappiness(data.getFloat(0));
        }
    }
```

9. Add the `setCountedThoughts` and `setAvgHappiness` methods. If the fragment is still attached to the activity, we will update the text view or the rating bar:

```
private void setCountedThoughts(final int counted){
    if (getActivity()==null){
        return;
    }
    getActivity().runOnUiThread(new Runnable() {
        @Override
        public void run() {
          TextView countText =
            (TextView)getView().findViewById(
              R.id.thoughts_kpi_count);
          countText.setText(String.valueOf(counted));
        }
    });
}
private void setAvgHappiness(final float avg){
    if (getActivity()==null){
        return;
    }
    getActivity().runOnUiThread(new Runnable() {
        @Override
        public void run() {
            RatingBar ratingBar =
              (RatingBar)getView().findViewById(
                R.id.thoughts_rating_bar_happy);
            ratingBar.setRating(avg);
        }
    });
}
```

10. In the `MainActivity` file, add a private member for the KPI fragment:

```
private ThoughtsKpiFragment mThoughtsKpiFragment;
```

11. Create a method `getKpiFragment`:

```
private ThoughtsKpiFragment getKpiFragment(){
    if (mThoughtsKpiFragment==null){
        mThoughtsKpiFragment = new ThoughtsKpiFragment();
    }
    return mThoughtsKpiFragment;
}
```

12. Locate the `onNavigationDraweItemSelected` method and add this to the `if` statement:

```
...
else if (position==0){
    fragmentManager.beginTransaction()
            .replace(R.id.container, getKpiFragment())
            .commit();
}
```

Run your app. Now we have some neat statistics in our thoughts app:

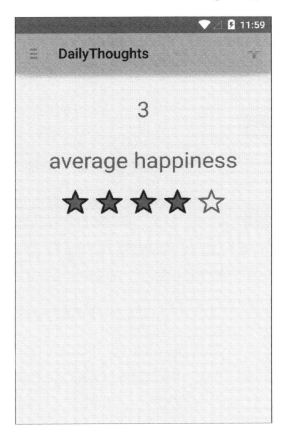

In this and in the previous recipe, we have seen how easy working with data becomes once you have grokked the concept of content providers.

So far we did all this within the same app; however, since we are already prepared to export the content provider, let us find out how to read our thoughts in a different app. Let's do that now.

See also

Refer *Chapter 5, Size Does Matter*

Refer *Chapter 8, Improving Quality*

Communicate with other apps using content providers

If you read Google's documentation about content providers, you will notice that a content provider basically is intended to supply data from one application to others on request. Such requests are handled by the methods of the `ContentResolver` class.

We will create a new app that will read our daily thoughts from the other one.

Getting ready

For this recipe, you need to have completed the previous one successfully. Make sure you have added some thoughts to your app as well or there'll be nothing to read otherwise, as Captain Obvious could tell us.

How to do it...

First we will create a new app. It is going to read our thoughts. That's for sure!

1. Create a new project in Android Studio, name it `DailyAnalytics`, and click on the **OK** button.

2. Select **Phone and tablet** and click on the **Next** button.

3. Choose **Blank Activity** and click on the **Next** button.

4. Accept all values in the **Customize the activity** view and click on the **Finish** button.

5. Open the `AndroidManifest.xml` file and add the permission required to communicate with the content provider from the `DailyThought` app:

    ```
    <uses-permission android:name=
      "com.packt.dailythoughts.READ_DATABASE"/>
    ```

6. Open the `activity_main.xml` layout and change the id of the `TextView` app to `main_kpi_count`:

    ```
    <TextView
        android:id="@+id/main_kpi_count"
        android:text="@string/hello_world"
        android:layout_width="wrap_content"
        android:layout_height="wrap_content" />
    ```

7. In the `MainActivity` class, add the `LoaderCallBack` implementation:

```
public class MainActivity extends Activity  implements
 LoaderManager.LoaderCallbacks<Cursor>
```

8. Call `initLoader` at the end of the `onCreate` method:

```
getLoaderManager().initLoader(0, null, this);
```

9. Add an implementation for the `onCreateLoader` method. It works pretty much in the same way as for the app the content provider is part of:

```
@Override
public Loader<Cursor> onCreateLoader(int id, Bundle args) {
    Uri uri = Uri.parse(
      "content://com.packt.dailythoughts/thoughts");
    String[] projection = new String[] { "_id", "name",
      "happiness"};
    String sortBy = "name";
    CursorLoader cursorLoader = new
    android.content.CursorLoader(
      this,uri, projection, null, null, null);
    return cursorLoader;
}
```

10. In the `onLoadFinished` method, we can display some analytics based on what you have entered in the other app:

```
@Override
public void onLoadFinished(Loader<Cursor> loader,
 Cursor data) {
   final StringBuilder builder = new StringBuilder();
    builder.append(
      "I know what you are thinking of... \n\n");
   while ( (data.moveToNext())){
       String onYourMind = data.getString(1);
       builder.append("You think of "+
         onYourMind+". ");
       if (data.getInt(2) <= 2){
          builder.append(
            "You are sad about this...");
        }
        if (data.getInt(2) >= 4) {
           builder.append("That makes you happy!");
        }
        builder.append("\n");
    }
    builder.append("\n Well, am I close? ;-)");
    runOnUiThread(new Runnable() {
```

```
        @Override
        public void run() {
          TextView countText = (TextView)
           findViewById(R.id.main_kpi_count);
          countText.setText(String.valueOf(
           builder.toString()));
        }
    });
}
```

Run the app and see all your thoughts appearing here as shown here:

Scary, isn't it? Using content providers, it is pretty easy to share data between different apps. This is how many apps such as contacts or the Gallery work.

There's more...

We have learned how content providers work, and we had a sneak peak at the observer pattern. Using this and other patterns could improve the quality of our app.

Now things will really become serious. Avoid potential errors, reduce the amount of code you need to write, and make it work on any Android device! We will find out how to do that in the next chapter.

See also

► Refer to *Chapter 8, Improving Quality*

8

Improving Quality

You have just finished coding your app. Now what? Get it onto the Play Store as quickly as possible!

No wait, you are not done yet! Did you test your app properly? Will it work on any Android version? On any device? In all circumstances?

In this chapter, we will focus on:

- ▶ Patterns and support annotations
- ▶ Unit testing using Robolectrics
- ▶ Code analysis

Introduction

There are some common pitfalls to avoid and some patterns that you may want to apply in order to improve the quality of your app. You have seen some of them in the previous chapters already. Also, there are some interesting tools that can be used to test and analyze your code.

In the following road map, you will notice that there are different stages that you need to complete before you can go live with your app:

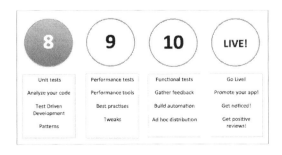

The structure of your code, robustness, maintainability, and how well it complies with the functional requirements are key elements.

Functional quality is measured through software testing, for which we need to distribute our app to our beta testers. We will discuss this in *Chapter 10, Beta Testing Your Apps*.

Structural quality is evaluated by running unit tests and code inspections manually (peer review) or using tools such as Android Lint, which you will learn more about in the final recipe within this chapter. Now the question is how well does the architecture of the code meet the demands of good software engineering?

In general, there are some interesting principles that will help you to improve the quality of your code. Some of them are listed here:

- Learn the activity lifecycle and use fragments in the right way.
- Don't allocate memory if it can be avoided.
- Avoid fragments and activities that are too heavy.
- Consider a **Model View Controller** (**MVC**) approach. Apply the correct patterns.
- Solve a problem once at a single spot. **Do not Repeat Yourself** (**DRY**).
- Don't do work that you do not need to do (yet). Also known as: **You Aren't Gonna Need It** (**YAGNI**).

The next recipe will give you an idea of what patterns are and why you would want to apply them.

Patterns and support annotations

Quality is a serious business so we will combine it with some fun. We will be creating a quiz app in the upcoming recipe. We will use Google Play services for this, and we will have a look at patterns that we can apply to our app, in particular the MVC and **Model View Presenter** (**MVP**) approach.

So what actually is a design pattern? A design pattern is a solution for a common problem. We can reuse such a pattern anywhere. There is no need to reinvent the wheel (unless you can think of a better one of course) and there is no need to repeat ourselves.

Patterns are best practices that we can trust on. They can help us to speed up the development process, including testing.

Some of the patterns are:

- MVC
- MVP
- Observable

- ▸ Factory
- ▸ Singleton
- ▸ Support annotations
- ▸ Google Play services

MVC

MVC is most suitable for larger projects. The benefit of this pattern is the separation of concerns. We can separate our UI code from the business logic. A controller will be responsible for which view is being displayed. It will get data from another layer, a repository-a-like class that will get its data from somewhere, and pass that data through a model (or list of models) to the UI. The controller has no clue where the data is coming from and how it is being displayed. These are tasks of the repository class and the UI, respectively.

MVP

MVP is a more suitable pattern to use with Android app development in most cases because of the nature of activities and fragments. With MVP patterns, a presenter contains the UI logic for a view. All invocations from the view are delegated directly to it. The presenter will communicate with the view through an interface, allowing us to create unit tests with mocked data later.

The observer pattern

We saw this pattern in *Chapter 7, Content Providers and Observers*, already. An observer observes changes in another object.

The factory pattern

This pattern helps to create an object. The bitmap factory that we have been using for previous recipes (and that we will use again in this recipe) is a great example of the factory pattern.

The singleton

The singleton pattern will prevent us from having multiple instances of an object. Typically, it is a (class) method that returns an instance. It will be created if it does not exist or else it will just return the previously created instance. The application class is an example of the singleton pattern.

Support annotations

Support annotations can help us to provide hints to code inspection tools, such as lint. They can help you detect problems such as null pointer exceptions and resource type conflicts just by adding metadata tags and running code inspections. The support library itself has been annotated with these annotations. Yes, they eat their own dog food, which proves that using annotations is the way to go.

There are basically three types of annotations that we can use: Nullness annotations, resource type annotations, and IntDef \ StringDef annotations. For example, we can use the `@NonNull` annotation to indicate that a given parameter cannot be null, or we can use the `@Nullable` annotation to indicate that a return value can be null.

Google Play services

The Play Games SDK provides cross-platform Google Play game services that let you easily integrate popular gaming features, such as achievements, leader boards, saved games, and real-time multiplayer (on Android) options in your tablet and mobile games.

That is enough theory for now! Let's create our Quiz app and apply some of the theory that we have discussed here.

Getting ready

For this recipe, you need to have the latest version of Android Studio and a real device on which Google Play services have been installed, which will be the case for most devices. Alternatively, you can install them on a virtual Genymotion device, but that will require some additional preparations.

Also, you need to have (or to create) a Google developer account.

How to do it...

And off we go. Start Android Studio and perform the following steps as we are going to build something great:

1. Create a new project in Android Studio. Name it `GetItRight` and click on the **Next** button.
2. Choose the **Phone and tablet** option and click on the **Next** button.
3. In the **Add an activity to mobile** view, choose **Google Play Service** and click on the **Next** button.
4. Accept the **activity name** and **title** fields and click on the **Finish** button.
5. Point your web browser at the Google Developer console and log in or register if you do not have an account yet. You can find it at: `https://console.developers.google.com`.
6. In the developer console, click on the game tab (game icon on the left-hand side of the webpage).
7. Accept the terms of service if asked to do so.
8. Click on the **Setup up Google Play Services** button.

9. Enter the name of the app `Get It Right Sample`, and pick a category: **Trivia**, and click on the **Continue** button.

10. In the game details view, enter a description and click on the **Save** button.

11. Next, you need to generate an Oauth2 client ID. To do so, click on the **Linked app** link.

12. Pick **Android** as your OS, enter `packt.com.getitright` as the **package name**, leave the other settings unchanged, and click on the **Save and continue** button.

13. Click on the **Authorize your app now** button in step 2. In the **Branding information** popup dialog, click on the **Continue** button.

14. The **Client ID** dialog appears. Enter `packt.com.getitright` as the package name. To get the signing certificate fingerprint, open **Terminal app** (for Windows: Command Prompt) and type:

```
keytool -exportcert -alias androiddebugkey -keystore ~/.android/
debug.keystore  -list -v
```

15. If asked for the `keystore` password, the default password for the debug keystore is `android`.

16. Copy and paste the fingerprint (SHA1) and click on the **Create Client** button.

17. Click on the **Back to the list** button, and after that click on the **Continue to next step** button.

18. In the **Android app details** view, you will see the **Application ID** (if you scroll down a little) that we are going to need later. Copy its value.

Leaderboards

Follow the given steps for adding leader boards to your app:

1. On the left-hand side of the webpage, choose **LEADERBOARDS** and click on the **Add new leaderboard** button. Name your new leaderboard `GetItRight Leaderboard` and click on the **Save** button. Note the leader board **ID**. We will be using it later:

2. Open the `build.gradle` file inside the `app` directory of your project and add a dependency for Google Play services:

    ```
    compile 'com.google.android.gms:play-services:7.5.0'
    ```

3. Sync your project. In case it fails to resolve Google Play services, an error will be generated including a link that reads **Install Repository and sync project**. Click on this link to do so.

4. Open the `AndroidManifest.xml` file and add a metadata tag to the application tag:

    ```
    <meta-data
      android:name="com.google.android.gms.games.APP_ID"
      android:value="@string/app_id" />
    ```

5. Also, add `app_id` to the `strings.xml` file:

    ```
    <resources>
        <string name="app_name">GetItRight</string>
        <string name="app_id">your app id</string>
    ```

6. Add a breakpoint on the first line of the `onConnected` method of the `GooglePlayServicesActivity` class. Do the same thing for the first line of the `onConnectionFailed` method. Using the Google Play service template and the provided app ID, you should be able to connect to Google Play Services already. Run the app (in debug mode) to find out if it does.

7. Create a new Android Resource directory and choose **layout** as the Resource type; create a new layout resource file within that directory and name it `activity_google_play_services.xml`.

8. Add some new strings to the `strings.xml` resource file:

    ```
    <string name="incorrect_answer">That is incorrect</string>
    <string name="correct_answer">That is the correct
     answer!</string>
    <string name="leader_board">LEADER BOARD</string>
    ```

9. Create a layout for the `activity_google_play_service` resource file:

    ```
    <?xml version="1.0" encoding="utf-8"?>
    <LinearLayout xmlns:android=
        "http://schemas.android.com/apk/res/android"
         android:orientation="vertical"
         android:layout_width="match_parent"
         android:padding="16dp"
         android:background="@android:color/holo_blue_dark"
         android:layout_height="match_parent">
         <ScrollView
           android:layout_width="match_parent"
           android:layout_height="wrap_content">
            <LinearLayout
               android:orientation="vertical"
    ```

```xml
            android:layout_width="match_parent"
            android:layout_height="wrap_content">
          <ImageView
            android:id="@+id/image"
            android:src=
              "@android:drawable/ic_popup_sync"
            android:layout_width="match_parent"
            android:layout_height="300px" />
          <TextView
            android:id="@+id/text"
            android:textColor="@android:color/white"
            android:text="Question"
            android:textSize="24sp"
            android:layout_width="match_parent"
            android:layout_height="wrap_content" />
          <LinearLayout
            android:orientation="vertical"
            android:layout_width="match_parent"
            android:layout_height="wrap_content">
          <Button
            android:id="@+id/button_1"
            android:layout_width="match_parent"
            android:layout_height="wrap_content"
            android:gravity="center_vertical|left" />
          <Button
            android:id="@+id/button_2"
            android:layout_width="match_parent"
            android:layout_height="wrap_content"
            android:gravity="center_vertical|left" />
          <Button
            android:id="@+id/button_3"
            android:layout_width="match_parent"
            android:layout_height="wrap_content"
            android:gravity="center_vertical|left" />
          <Button
            android:id="@+id/button_4"
            android:layout_width="match_parent"
            android:layout_height="wrap_content"
            android:gravity="center_vertical|left" />
          <Button
            android:id="@+id/button_test"
            android:text="@string/leader_board"
            android:layout_width="match_parent"
            android:layout_height="wrap_content"
            android:gravity="center_vertical|left" />
          </LinearLayout>
        </LinearLayout>
      </ScrollView>
</LinearLayout>
```

10. Open the `GooglePlayServicesActivity` file. In the `onCreate` method, load the layout and set the on click listeners for all buttons:

```
setContentView(R.layout.activity_google_play_services);
findViewById(R.id.button_1).setOnClickListener(this);
findViewById(R.id.button_2).setOnClickListener(this);
findViewById(R.id.button_3).setOnClickListener(this);
findViewById(R.id.button_4).setOnClickListener(this);
findViewById(R.id.button_test).setOnClickListener(this);
```

11. Implement the `onClickListener` method for the `GooglePlayServicesActivity` file. Android Studio will suggest an implementation and you can accept this suggestion or add the implementation yourself:

```
public class GooglePlayServicesActivity extends Activity
implements GoogleApiClient.ConnectionCallbacks,
  GoogleApiClient.OnConnectionFailedListener,
    View.OnClickListener {
@Override
public void onClick(View v) {
}
```

12. Add two private members, one for our leaderboard request and one that will hold your leaderboard ID:

```
private int REQUEST_LEADERBOARD = 1;
private String LEADERBOARD_ID = "<your leaderboard id>";
```

13. Create the implementation for the `onClick` method. We are preparing the situation where the user clicks on any of the multiple choice options. For the **leaderboard** (test) button, we can add the implementation right away:

```
@Override
public void onClick(View v) {
    switch (v.getId()){
        case R.id.button_1:
        case R.id.button_2:
        case R.id.button_3:
        case R.id.button_4:
            break;
        case R.id.button_test:
         startActivityForResult(
          Games.Leaderboards.getLeaderboardIntent(
            mGoogleApiClient, LEADERBOARD_ID),
             REQUEST_LEADERBOARD);
          break;
    }
}
```

14. Create a new package and name it `models`. Create the `Answer`, `Question`, and `Quiz` classes:

    To add the `Answer` class, you need the following code:

```
public class Answer {
    private String mId;
    private String mText;
    public String getId() {
        return mId;
    }
    public String getText() {
        return mText;
    }
    public Answer (String id, String text) {
        mId = id;
        mText = text;
    }
}
```

To add the `Question` class, use the given code:

```
public class Question {
    private String mText;
    private String mUri;
    private String mCorrectAnswer;
    private String mAnswer;
    private ArrayList<Answer> mPossibleAnswers;
    public String getText(){
        return mText;
    }
    public String getUri(){
        return mUri;
    }
    public String getCorrectAnswer(){
        return mCorrectAnswer;
    }
    public String getAnswer(){
        return mAnswer;
    }
    public Question (String text, String uri, String
     correctAnswer){
        mText = text;
        mUri = uri;
        mCorrectAnswer = correctAnswer;
    }
    public Answer addAnswer(String id, String text){
```

```
        if (mPossibleAnswers==null){
            mPossibleAnswers = new ArrayList<Answer>();
        }
        Answer answer = new Answer(id,text);
        mPossibleAnswers.add(answer);
        return answer;
    }
    public ArrayList<Answer> getPossibleAnswers(){
        return mPossibleAnswers;
    }
}
```

To add the `Quiz` class, use the following code:

```
public class Quiz {
    private ArrayList<Question> mQuestions;
    public ArrayList<Question> getQuestions(){
        return mQuestions;
    }
    public Question addQuestion(String text, String uri, String
     correctAnswer){
        if (mQuestions==null){
            mQuestions = new ArrayList<Question>();
        }
        Question question = new Question(
         text,uri,correctAnswer);
        mQuestions.add(question);
        return question;
    }
}
```

15. Create a new package and name it `repositories`. Create a new class and name it `QuizRepository`. Add some questions to the quiz. You can use the questions from the following example, but you can create some questions yourself as well if you would like to do so. In a real app, the questions and answers, of course, would not be hardcoded but retrieved from a database or from a backend (note that we can always change this behavior later without the need to modify anything but this class):

```
public class QuizRepository {
    public Quiz getQuiz(){
      Quiz quiz = new Quiz();
      Question q1 = quiz.addQuestion(
       "1. What is the largest city in the world?",
        "http://cdn.acidcow.com/pics/20100923/
        skylines_of_large_cities_05.jpg" , "tokyo");
        q1.addAnswer("delhi" , "Delhi, India");
        q1.addAnswer("tokyo" , "Tokyo, Japan");
```

```
q1.addAnswer("saopaulo" , "Sao Paulo, Brazil");
q1.addAnswer("nyc" , "New York, USA");
Question q2 = quiz.addQuestion("2. What is the
largest animal in the world?",
"http://www.onekind.org/uploads/a-
  z/az_aardvark.jpg" , "blue_whale");
q2.addAnswer("african_elephant" , "African
Elephant");
q2.addAnswer("brown_bear" , "Brown Bear");
q2.addAnswer("giraffe" , "Giraffe");
q2.addAnswer("blue_whale" , "Blue whale");
Question q3 = quiz.addQuestion("3. What is the
highest mountain in the world?",
 "http://images.summitpost.org/medium/
815426.jpg", "mount_everest");
q3.addAnswer("mont_blanc" , "Mont Blanc");
q3.addAnswer("pico_bolivar" , "Pico Bolívar");
q3.addAnswer("mount_everest" , "Mount Everest");
q3.addAnswer("kilimanjaro" , "Mount
Kilimanjaro");
return quiz;
    }
}
```

16. In the `GamePlayServicesActivity` class, add these three private members:

```
private Quiz mQuiz;
private int mScore;
private int mQuestionIndex=0;
```

17. Add the implementation for the `newGame` method. We will get the `Quiz` object by asking the repository for it. After resetting the score and the question index, we call the `displayQuestion` method, which implements the UI logic by actually displaying the question, the possible answers, and a nice image:

```
private void newGame(){
    mQuiz = new QuizRepository().getQuiz();
    mScore = 0;
    mQuestionIndex = 0;
    displayQuestion(mQuiz.getQuestions().get(mQuestionIndex));
}
private void displayQuestion(Question question){
    TextView questionText = (TextView)findViewById(R.id.text);
    displayImage(question);
    questionText.setText(question.getText());
    ArrayList<Answer> answers = question.getPossibleAnswers();
    setPossibleAnswer(findViewById(R.id.button_1),
     answers.get(0));
    setPossibleAnswer(findViewById(R.id.button_2),
```

```
            answers.get(1));
        setPossibleAnswer(findViewById(R.id.button_3),
         answers.get(2));
        setPossibleAnswer(findViewById(R.id.button_4),
         answers.get(3));
    }
    private void setPossibleAnswer(View v, Answer answer){
        if (v instanceof Button) {
            ((Button) v).setText(answer.getText());
            v.setTag(answer);
        }
    }
    private void displayImage(final Question question){
        new Thread(new Runnable() {
            public void run(){
                try {
                    URL url = new URL(question.getUri());
                    final Bitmap image = BitmapFactory.decodeStream(
                     url.openConnection().getInputStream());
                    runOnUiThread(new Runnable() {
                        @Override
                        public void run() {
                            ImageView imageView = (ImageView)
                                findViewById(R.id.image);
                            imageView.setImageBitmap(image);
                        }
                    });
                }
                catch (Exception ex){
                    Log.d(getClass().toString(), ex.getMessage());
                }
            }
        }).start();
    }
```

Let the game begin!

The following steps can be used to add methods to a new game:

1. At the end of the `onCreate` method, we will call the `newGame` method:

   ```
   newGame();
   ```

2. Modify the `onClick` method, so we can respond when a user clicks on any of the buttons. If any of the multiple choice buttons are being clicked on, we will call the `checkAnswer` method. Is it the correct answer we have chosen? How exciting:

   ```
   @Override
   public void onClick(View v) {
       switch (v.getId()){
   ```

```
        case R.id.button_1:
        case R.id.button_2:
        case R.id.button_3:
        case R.id.button_4:
            checkAnswer(v);
            break;
        case R.id.button_test: startActivityForResult(
         Games.Leaderboards.getLeaderboardIntent(
          mGoogleApiClient, LEADERBOARD_ID),
           REQUEST_LEADERBOARD);

        break;
    }
}
```

3. Add the `checkAnswer` method. We will compare the given answer against the correct answer for the question, and depending on the result, we will call the `onGoodAnswer` or `onWrongAnswer` methods. Depending on the answer, your progress gets decided: if the answer is wrong, the game is over and we display the leader board.

4. If there are no more questions, we will submit the users score and display the leader board as well. The leader board itself will take care of all the logic for it. Was the submitted score high enough to make your name appear on top of the list? Check it with the help of the following snippet:

```
private void checkAnswer(View v){
    if (v instanceof Button){
        Answer answer = (Answer)((Button)v).getTag();
        if (mQuiz.getQuestions().get(mQuestionIndex).
         getCorrectAnswer().equalsIgnoreCase(
          answer.getId())){
            onGoodAnswer();
        }
        else{
            onWrongAnswer();
        }
    }
}
private void onWrongAnswer(){
    Toast.makeText(this, getString(
     R.string.incorrect_answer), Toast.LENGTH_SHORT).show();
    startActivityForResult(
     Games.Leaderboards.getLeaderboardIntent(
     mGoogleApiClient, LEADERBOARD_ID),
```

```
            REQUEST_LEADERBOARD);
    }
    private void onGoodAnswer(){
        mScore+= 1000;
        Games.Leaderboards.submitScore(mGoogleApiClient,
         LEADERBOARD_ID, mScore);
        Toast.makeText(this, getString(R.string.correct_answer),
         Toast.LENGTH_SHORT).show();
        mQuestionIndex++;
        if (mQuestionIndex < mQuiz.getQuestions().size()){
            displayQuestion(mQuiz.getQuestions().get(
             mQuestionIndex));
        }
        else{
            startActivityForResult(
             Games.Leaderboards.getLeaderboardIntent(
              mGoogleApiClient, LEADERBOARD_ID),
               REQUEST_LEADERBOARD);
        }
    }
}
```

5. To be prepared for unit testing and code inspection let's add annotation support. Open the `build.gradle` file in the `app` folder and add the dependency. Click on the **Sync now** link that appears after modifying the file:

```
compile 'com.android.support:support-annotations:22.2.0'
```

6. If an error appears that reads `Failed to resolve support-annotations`, then click on the **Install Repository and Sync Project** link that appears.

7. If all goes well, then we can add annotations, for example, to the parameter of the `CheckAnswer` method:

```
private void checkAnswer(@NonNull View v){
```

8. In the `Question` class, we could add a `@Nullable` annotation to the `getPossibleAnswers` method, which could be the case if we did not provide any multiple choice option for a question:

```
@Nullable
public ArrayList<Answer> getPossibleAnswers(){
    return mPossibleAnswers;
}
```

9. Later, if we do some analysis, this will result in a warning for `GooglePlayServiceActivity`, where we will be calling this method. We will have a closer look at that in the *code analysis* recipe:

```
Method invocation 'answers.get(0)' may produce  'java.lang.
NullPointerException'
```

You can play the game if you like and add some more annotations. Just don't play too long with them. Let's play the game instead!

Run your app and become number one on the leader board. Since currently you are the only test player, that cannot be too hard I guess.

You have just created your own quiz app, which you can extend with some other challenging questions if you like, as shown in the following screenshot:

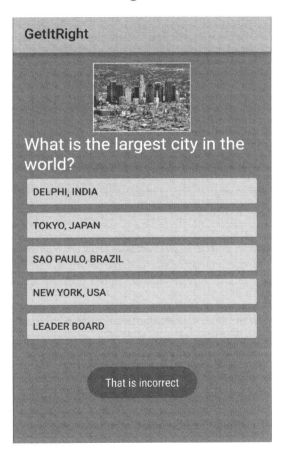

We have investigated Google Play services and we have been using a MVC approach for our app. Also, we had a look at how to use annotations, which could help us to improve code after doing some code analysis.

There's more...

We had only a sneak peek at patterns and how to apply them. Check out the Internet or get some great books to learn more about patterns. Also, refer to `https://www.google.com/design/spec/patterns/app-structure.html`.

Make sure you read the docs about support annotations as well. There are so many more possibilities using them. Check the docs out at `http://tools.android.com/tech-docs/support-annotations`.

Also, we have been using Google Play services for only a fraction. We just know how to sign in and how to use a leader board. If you want, you can check out the other options. For that, refer to `https://developers.google.com/games/services/android/quickstart`.

See also

▸ Refer to *Chapter 7, Content Providers and Observers*.

Unit testing using Robolectric

Unit testing is a testing method where individual units of code are tested. A view or repository can be tested, for example, to check whether it meets the demands. Unlike most other tests, these kinds of tests typically are developed and run by a software developer.

Ideally, a test case is completely independent from other cases and other units. Since classes often depend on others substitutes such as mock objects needs to be used. In the previous recipe, the `QuizRepository` class provides hardcoded quiz data (stubbed or mocked data), but as suggested, the intention is that the quiz data should be retrieved from a backend.

We are going to prepare the app we created in the previous recipe for unit testing, and we will create some tests ourselves. **Robolectric** is going to help us with that. Although since the 1.2 release of Android Studio unit testing (based on JUnit) has become much easier to set up, it still is not as powerful as Robolectric.

Robolectric does not need additional mock frameworks and it can be run outside the emulator as well, allowing us to combine unit testing with a continuous integration environment, as we are going to do in *Chapter 10, Beta Testing Your Apps*.

Getting ready

For this recipe, it would be most ideal to have the previous recipe successfully completed. In case you prefer to skip that part of this chapter, you can, of course, open your own project and set up unit testing in more or less the same way. That is up to you.

How to do it...

So what do we have to do to create and run some unit tests? Let's find out:

1. Open the project that we created in the previous recipe.

2. Open the `build.gradle` file within the `app` folder and add a dependency for Robolectric:

   ```
   testCompile 'org.robolectric:robolectric:3.0'
   ```

3. Rename the `androidTest` folder in the `src` folder to `test`.

4. From the **Run** menu choose the **Edit configurations** option.

5. On the left-hand side of Run\Debug Configuration window, choose **Defaults** and **JUnit**. On the right-hand side change the content for **Working directory** to `$MODULE_DIR$` and click on the **OK** button.

6. Rename the **ApplicationTest** class to `QuizRepositoryTest`.

7. Add some tests to the **QuizRepositoryTest** class. We will be using Robolectric for this. As you can notice, we will be using annotations here as well just like we did in the previous recipe:

   ```java
   @Config(constants = BuildConfig.class, sdk = 21)
   @RunWith(RobolectricGradleTestRunner.class)
   public class QuizRepositoryTest {
       private QuizRepository mRepository;
       @Before
       public void setup() throws Exception {
           mRepository = new QuizRepository();
           assertNotNull("QuizRepository is not
           instantiated", mRepository);
       }
       @Test
       public void quizHasQuestions() throws Exception {
           Quiz quiz = mRepository.getQuiz();
           ArrayList<Question> questions = quiz.getQuestions();
           assertNotNull("quiz could not be created", quiz);

           assertNotNull("quiz contains no questions",
            questions);
           assertTrue("quiz contains no questions",
   ```

```
            questions.size()>0);
    }
    @Test
    public void quizHasSufficientQuestions() throws
     Exception {
        Quiz quiz = mRepository.getQuiz();
        ArrayList<Question> questions = quiz.getQuestions();
        assertNotNull("quiz could not be created", quiz);

        assertNotNull("quiz contains no questions",
         questions);

        assertTrue("quiz contains insufficient
        questions", questions.size()>=10);
    }
}
```

8. Create another test class so we can test the activity. Name the new class
    `GooglePlayServicesActivityTest`. Within this test, we could perform
    some layout tests as well:

```
@Config(constants = BuildConfig.class, sdk = 21)
@RunWith(RobolectricGradleTestRunner.class)
public class GooglePlayServicesActivityTest {
    private GooglePlayServicesActivity activity;
    @Before
    public void setup() throws Exception {
        activity = Robolectric.setupActivity(
         GooglePlayServicesActivity.class);
        assertNotNull("GooglePlayServicesActivity is not
        instantiated", activity);
    }
    @Test
    public void testButtonExistsAndHasCorrectText() throws
    Exception {
        Button testButton = (Button) activity.findViewById(
         R.id.button_test);
        assertNotNull("testButton could not be found",
         testButton);
        assertTrue("testButton contains wrong text",
         activity.getString( R.string.leader_board).equals(
         testButton.getText().toString()));
    }
}
```

9. Open the `build variants` pane and choose `Unit tests` instead of
    `Instrumentation tests`.

Everything under the `test` package will be highlighted in green now (you may need to do a rebuild first). If you right-click on the package name `packt.com.getitright` or on any of the test classes you created, you will find an option in the context menu **Run tests in packt.com.getright** or **Run QuizRepositoryTest**. For example, choose to run `QuizRepositoryTest`. If you choose this option, Gradle starts thinking for a bit. After a while, the results are displayed.

Only the tests that fail are shown by default. To see the tests that did succeed as well, click on the **Hide passed** button (the button above the test tree shown on the left-hand side).

You will see that the **quizHasQuestions** test has passed. However, the **quizHasSufficientQuestions** test has failed. This makes sense, as our test requires our quiz to have at least 10 questions while we added only three to the quiz, as shown in the following figure:

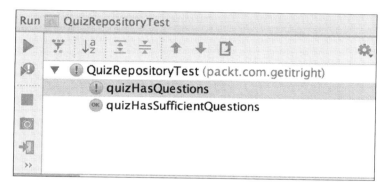

Add seven more questions to `Quiz` in `QuizRepository` to get it right. Well, you can cheat, of course, by modifying the test, but let's just say it is a business requirement.

Rerun the test. Every unit test succeeded. Hurrah! Create a few more unit tests that you can think of.

Unit testing is a very interesting option because we can use it for continuous integration purposes as well. Think of a scenario where we run the unit tests each time you commit (and push) your source to a central repository such as GitHub or BitBucket. If the compilation and all unit tests succeed, we can create a new (ad hoc) release automatically or be notified whether the compilation or any of the tests failed.

There's more...

There are plenty of other tools and approaches available for mobile testing purposes.

In addition to unit testing, we want to test the **User Interface** (**UI**) as well, for example, by using Espresso.

Espresso

Espresso is suitable for writing concise and reliable Android UI tests. A test typically contains clicks, text input, and checks. It is actually pretty simple to write tests. The following is an example of a test using Espresso:

```
@Test
public void testLogin() {
    onView(withId(R.id.login)).perform(
     typeText("mike@test.com"));
    onView(withId(R.id.greet_button)).perform(click());
}
```

To quote the website:

"Espresso tests state expectations, interactions, and assertions clearly without the distraction of boilerplate content, custom infrastructure, or messy implementation details getting in the way".

For more information, refer to `https://code.google.com/p/android-test-kit/ wiki/Espresso`.

Approaches

When it comes to testing, there are different approaches you can think of. One of these approaches is **Test-driven Development** (**TDD**). If the functionality and all requirements are known, we can define our tests before developing our app. Of course, all tests will fail initially, but that is actually a good thing. It will set an outline of what needs to be done and create focus to get things right. If you start developing more and more, tests will succeed, remaining the amount of work.

Another and more recent approach is **Behavior-driven Development** (**BDD**). This testing approach is based around features, where a feature is a collection of stories expressed from a particular point of view.

BDD tools come as a unit testing flavor such as `Rspec` for example and as a higher level acceptance testing flavor: `Cucumber`.

Cucumber, Gherkin, and Calabash

No, this is not a greengrocer advertisement that suddenly has popped up here. **Cucumber** is a tool that runs automated acceptance tests written in a BDD style. It allows the execution of a feature documentation written in a business-facing text.

Here is an example of a feature file using **Gherkin**. It serves two purposes: documentation and automated tests:

```
Scenario: Login
  Given I am on the Login Screen
  Then I touch the "Email" input field
  Then I use the keyboard and type "test@packt.com"
  Then I touch the "Password" input field
  Then I use the keyboard and type "verysecretpassword"
  Then I touch "LOG IN"
  Then I should see "Hello world"
```

Gherkin is a business-readable, domain-specific language that lets you describe a software's behavior without detailing on how that behavior is implemented. Therefore, these tests can also be written by the nondeveloping members of your team.

There is some glue code required to make things happen. In Cucumber, this process is defined in step definitions. Cucumber typically lets you write these step definitions in the Ruby language.

Through the Calabash framework, you can use Cucumber to create tests for both Android and iOS. It enables you to define and execute automated acceptance tests. Another great thing about Calabash is that it allows you to run automated tests on the cloud, for example, using the services of TestDroid.

First things first!

To learn more about Cucumber, visit https://cucumber.io.

You will find the Calabash framework at http://calaba.sh.

Also, check out www.testdroid.com for more information about testing on as many devices as possible using TestDroid a cloud based test environment.

Finally, find a good balance between time, quality, and money. The approach to test your app depends on how valuable you (or your company or your customer) think each of these elements are. Create at least unit and UI tests. Also, let's not forget about performance testing, but that a topic that will be discussed in the next chapter!

See also

- Refer to *Chapter 9, Improving Performance*
- Refer to *Chapter 10, Beta Testing Your Apps*

Code analysis

Code analysis tools, such as Android Lint, can help you detect potential bugs and how your app can be optimized for security, usability, and performance.

Android Lint comes with Android Studio, but there are also other tools available such as: Check Style, **Project Mess Detector** (**PMD**), and Find Bugs. In this recipe, we will only have a look at Android Lint.

Getting ready

> ▶ Most ideally, you would have completed the first two recipes of this chapter, so we will now examine the results of the app. However, you can use `Android Lint` (or another tool) on any project to see where things can be improved.

 The support annotations of the first recipe influence the results being displayed. Yes, that is right, we cause these warnings.

How to do it...

There is nothing that we need to install in order to get an Android Lint report, as it is already in there with Android Studio. Just follow the next steps to make use of it:

1. Open the project you have created in the previous recipes. Or, alternatively, open your own project.

2. From the **Analyze** menu, choose **Code inspection**. The inspection scope is the whole project. Click on the **OK** button to proceed.

3. The results for inspection will be presented as a tree view. Expand and select items to see what each item is about, as shown in the following snapshot:

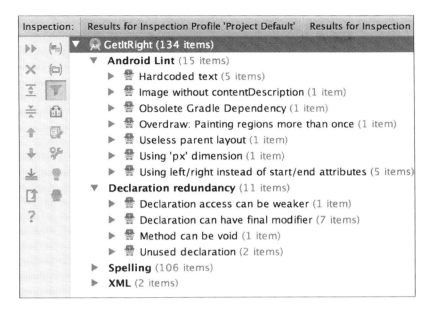

4. Things look pretty serious here but actually, it is not all that bad. There are some issues that are no show stoppers at all, but fixing them could greatly improve your code, which is what we are aiming at for now.

5. For example, check out the **Declaration redundancy** | **Declaration access can be weaker** | **Can be private** issue. Navigate to it. Double-click on it to jump to the code where the issue appears. Right-click on it. The context menu provides a solution for this right away. Choose the **Make field private** option to apply the correct solution. If you do so, this item will be marked as done (strike-through).

6. Now have a look at **Hardcoded texts**. If you double-click on any of the items that are related to this issue, you will see what the problem is.

7. For our convenience, we did put a temporary text (such as `Question` in `Text View`). If this was for real, we should be using a string resource instead. Here, we can safely remove the text. If you rerun the code inspection, the issue will disappear:

```
<TextView
    android:id="@+id/text"
    android:textColor="@android:color/white"
    android:textSize="24sp"
    android:layout_width="match_parent"
    android:layout_height="wrap_content" />
```

8. Next, have a look at **Constant conditions & exceptions** under **Probable bugs**. For the `GooglePlayServicesActivity` file, it says:

```
Method invocation 'answers.get(0)' may produce 'java.lang.
NullPointerException'
```

9. If you double-click on this message, you will find what the issue is about:

```
setPossibleAnswer(findViewById(R.id.button_1), answers.get(0));
```

10. This line may produce `Null Pointer Exception` Why is that? If you go to the declaration of the `getPossibleAnswers` method by selecting it and pressing *Cmd + B* (for Windows: *Ctrl + B*) you will find out why:

```
@Nullable
public ArrayList<Answer> getPossibleAnswers(){
    return mPossibleAnswers;
}
```

Ah right! We added this annotation ourselves in the first recipe to remind our later selves (or fellow developer) that the answers that are returned might be null. There are a couple of ways to fix this.

11. We could remove the `@Nullable` annotation here, but that would be bad since the answers actually could be null. We also could choose to suppress the warning.

12. The best solution is to actually test the outcome of the `getAnswers` method before doing anything with it. Just like that:

```
ArrayList<Answer> answers = question.getPossibleAnswers();
if (answers == null){
    return;
}
```

13. Expand **Declaration redundancy | Method can be void | Question**. It says:

Return value of the method is never used

14. Double-click on the issue to jump the code. Well, that warning is correct but suppose I do want to return the answer any way because I am pretty sure (how sure can you be?) I will be consuming it later. In that case, you could right-click on the issue and choose the **Suppress for Member** option. You will not be bothered by this issue again because it will add the `SuppressWarnings` annotation to your code:

```
@SuppressWarnings("UnusedReturnValue")
public Answer addAnswer(String id, String text){
```

15. Finally, have a look at **Spelling warnings**. Expand **Spelling** and the underlying **Typo** and **app** items. There it is. A `Typo`!

Typo: In word 'getitright'

We didn't get **getitright** right now did we? Since it is the name of our app and because it is part of the package name, I am pretty sure we can safely ignore this warning. This time, we right-click on the type and choose the **Save to dictionary** option:

16. The list of warnings seems to be endless, but how severe are all these items? On the left-hand side of Android Studio, you will find a button with the **Group by Severity** tooltip. Click on it.

17. Now the tree view contains an error node (if you have any), a warning node, and a typo node. If you just concentrate on the errors and warnings and see what each item is about, then you will improve your code and actually learn quite a lot, as each issue comes with a description of the problem and a suggestion on how to fix it.

Great, you learned some cool stuff today! And wrote better code by applying patterns, running unit tests, and by fixing issues reported by `Android Lint`.

We now know that our app does what it should do and that it is well structured after some refactoring.

The next thing to wonder about is what would happen if the images we are loading from the Internet are 10 times the size they are now? What if we have 1000 questions? Unreal? Perhaps.

How will our Quiz app perform on a low-end device? In the next chapter, we will go after the answers to these and other questions.

See also

> Refer to *Chapter 9, Performance*
> Refer to *Chapter 10, Beta Testing Your App*

9
Improving Performance

Performance matters as it has an impact on the reviews your app gets on the Google Play Store. A five-star app is what we want! On a high-end device, your app might be running smoothly without any trouble, but on a user's low-end device, things might look a little bit different. It performs slowly or runs out of memory, resulting in the crashing of that app.

In this chapter, you will learn the following recipes:

- ▶ Memory profilers and performance tools
- ▶ Here comes the bad app—performance improvements
- ▶ Overdraw issues

Introduction

How can we detect whether there will be any performance issues with our app? What are the common problems in Android apps? And how can we fix these issues?

When it comes to performance, a few problems that could occur are as follows:

▸ **Memory leaks**: Although Android comes with its own memory management system, memory leaks may occur.

▸ **Out of memory exceptions**: Your app could easily run out of memory, resulting in a crash of your app. For example, think of processing large images on low-end devices.

▸ **Overdraw**: Overdraw is the phenomenon of a pixel on a view being drawn more than once. It can result in an unresponsive or laggy user interface.

In the upcoming recipes, we will examine the problems listed here. The Android SDK and Android Studio come with some great tools to examine your app.

Memory profilers and performance tools

Your app could suffer from memory leaks or from allocating too much memory.

The **Garbage Collector** (**GC**), responsible for cleaning up anything we do not want to use any more, is a great helper, but unfortunately, it is not perfect. It can only remove objects that are recognized as unreachable. Objects that are not cleaned up just hang around taking up space. After a while, if more and more objects are created, an `OutOfMemoryError` could occur, as would be the case if a couple of large images are attempted to load, which is a commonly seen crash scenario for many Android apps.

Memory leaks are somewhat difficult to find. Luckily for us, Android Studio comes with a memory monitor. It gives you an overview of your app's memory usage and some clue about memory leaks.

We will be using this **Memory monitor** to find out whether unwanted GC event patterns are causing performance issues. In addition to this, we will use **Allocation Tracker** to identify where in the code the problem might be.

Getting ready

For this recipe, it would be great if you have completed any of the recipes from the previous chapters. If possible, it should be the recipe that consumes data (text and images) from the Internet, for example, the app from *Chapter 2, Applications with a Cloud-based Backend*. Of course, any other app will do, as we are going to examine tools that will inspect our app in order to improve it.

How to do it...

Let's find out how well our app performs!

1. Start Android Studio and open the app of your choice.

2. Run your app on a device (or use a virtual Genymotion device).

3. The **Memory monitor** is situated on the **Memory** tab, which you can find on the **Android** tab.

4. If it is not shown, use the *Cmd + 6* (for Windows: *Alt + 6*) shortcut to make it appear.

5. Run your app to see the memory monitor recording your app's memory usage. In the following example, I have run an app that loads 200 venues (containing text and images) from the FourSquare API. I request 200 more of them each time I press the button, resulting in the peaks shown in this graph. Give me more coffee shops in my neighborhood, please:

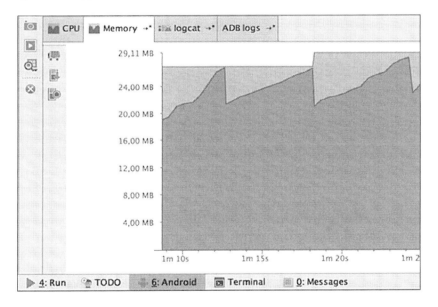

6. The app's memory usage is displayed in dark blue. The unallocated memory appears in light blue. The allocated memory will grow when your app starts performing until there is no more memory left, or it will drop when the GC has arrived and done its job.

7. These are common events, and eventually, you call the GC yourself by clicking on the **Initiate GC** icon (the button on the upper-left corner of the **Memory** tab) on the left-hand side of the window.

8. It will only be suspicious if a lot of memory is allocated in a short period of time or if the GC events occur more often. Your app may have a memory leak.

9. In the same way, you can monitor the CPU usage. You can find it on the **CPU** tab on the **Android** panel. If you notice very high peaks here, your app might be doing too much. In the following screenshot everything looks just fine:

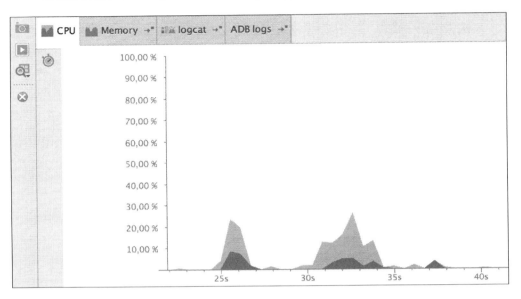

10. To learn more about memory issues, we can use another tool. From the **Tools** menu, choose **Android** and the **Android Device Monitor** option. This tool comes with a heap view, memory monitor, and allocation tracker, which are all tools that provide insight on the memory that your app uses.

11. If it is not selected yet, click on the **Dalvik Debug Monitor Server** (**DDMS**) button that appears on the top navigator bar. DDMS is a debugging tool that provides thread and heap information and a couple of other things.

12. Select the **Heap** tab. On the right-hand side of the window, select your running app that should appear right under the device name. If you do not see your app, you might need to rerun your app.

13. Memory requests will be handled by allocating parts from a pool of memory, which is called a heap. At any given time, some parts of the heap are in use, while some are unused and therefore available for future allocations.

14. The **Heap** tab can help you diagnose memory leaks by displaying how much memory the system has allocated for your app. Here, you can identify object types that get or stay allocated unexpectedly or unnecessarily. If the allocated memory keeps on increasing, then this is a strong indication that your app has a memory leak.

> If heap updates are not enabled, check out the buttons on the **Devices** tab. Click on the **update Heap** button (second from the left-hand side of the screenshot).

15. The heap output is displayed only after a GC event. On the heap tab, find the **Cause GC** button and click on it to force the GC to do its job. After this, the **heap** tab will look somewhat like this:

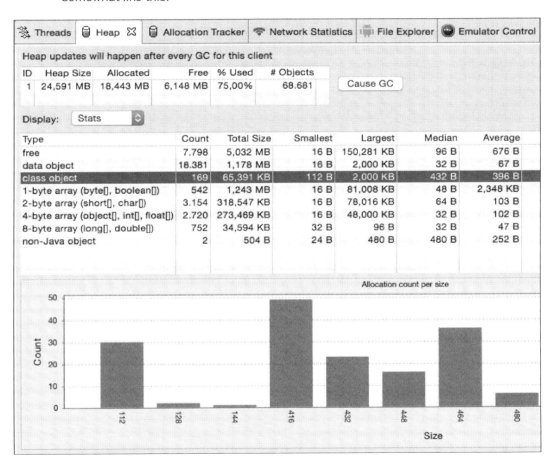

16. A lot of information about the app's heap usage is displayed in the preceding screenshot. Click on any item in the table to get further information. The information shown here can help you identify which parts of your app are causing too many allocations. Perhaps, you need to reduce the number of allocations or release memory earlier.

17. To better understand what the critical parts of your app are and what stack trace exactly is causing the issues, you can click on the **Allocation Tracker** tab.

18. On that tab, click on the **Start Tracking** button.

19. Interact with your app in some way by refreshing the list, going to a detail view or whatever it is that your app does and that you would like to measure.

20. Click on the **Get allocations** button to update the list of allocations.

21. As a result of the operation that you have initiated for your app, you will see all the recent allocations listed here.

22. To see the stack trace, click on any of the allocations. In the example shown next, we are investigating the loading of an image within a table row. The trace shows what type of object was allocated in which thread, and where.

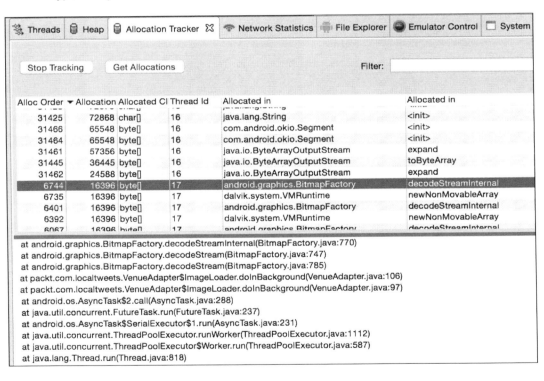

If you like, you can play around a little bit to learn more about the Android device monitor. Now that you have seen some of the tools to measure results, let's have a closer look at how to deal with them and how we can avoid memory issues. See you at the next recipe!

There's more...

Both the **Android Device Monitor** and the memory tools that come with Android Studio have many more options that you could explore. These options will help you improve the quality and performance of your app. It will make you and your app users happy!

See also

- ▶ *Chapter 2, Applications with a Cloud-based Backend*
- ▶ *Chapter 8, Improve Quality*
- ▶ *Chapter 10, Beta Testing Your App*

Here comes the bad app – performance improvements

What are the do's and don'ts for Android application development to avoid performance issues, even if they may not occur on your own device? Testing Android apps is hard because there are so many devices out there. It is better to be safe than sorry, so write your code carefully.

Some say that there are two basic rules to writing efficient code: don't do the work that you don't need to do (hence the DRY and YAGNI principles from *Chapter 8, Improving Quality*) and do not allocate memory if you can avoid it. In addition to this, it is also interesting to know that there are various libraries available that will not just save you the time but also prove to be very efficient. Of course, reinventing the wheel could be error prone as well.

Think of the `RetroFit` library, for example, that will make it much easier to write code to consume web services, or think of `Picasso`, an image loading library that will load an image from a URL with just one line of code without worrying too much about things such as threading, image sizing, transforming, or memory management.

In general, some good practices are as follows:

- ▶ Optimize bitmap memory usage.
- ▶ Release memory when hiding the user interface.
- ▶ Do not use too many nested views in your layouts.
- ▶ Do not create unnecessary objects, classes, or inner classes.
- ▶ Use primitive types instead of objects where possible.

▸ Prefer static methods over virtual methods if you do not need any of the members of an object. Static invocations will be faster.

▸ Try to avoid internal getters and setters, as direct field access is much faster in Android.

▸ Do not use floating points if integers can do the trick.

▸ If you register a listener, then make sure you also unregister it. Register and unregister in the corresponding pairs of the activity lifecycle. Register, for example, in the `onCreate` method and unregister in the `onDestroy` method. Or, register in the `onResume` method and unregister in the `onPause` method.

▸ Provide feedback to the user if an operation takes more time than a few seconds. Let the user know that your app is not dead but busy! Show that something is going on by showing a progress indicator.

▸ Always measure. Use performance tools to find out how well your app is doing.

Android Studio tip

Are you looking for something? Press *Shift* two times and start typing what you're searching for. Or, to display all the recent files, use the *Cmd + E* (for Windows: *Ctrl + E*) shortcut.

Getting ready

For this recipe, you just need to have Android Studio up and running and preferably a real device with Internet access.

How to do it...

Let's create a really bad application so we have something to fix. We will not optimize bitmap memory usage. We will use nested views a lot, do a couple of other really bad things, and for this recipe, we will display a list of the worst movies ever. Here comes the bad app:

1. Create a new project in Android Studio.

2. Name it `BadApp` and click on the **Next** button.

3. Check the **Phone and Tablet** option and click on the **Next** button.

4. Choose **Blank Activity** and click on the **Next** button.

5. Accept the names as is and click on the **Finish** button.

6. Open the `activity_main.xml` layout and replace the content with a list view that has a nice background color within a relative layout that has another nice background color. We are doing this because we want to demonstrate the overview issue in the next recipe:

```xml
<RelativeLayout xmlns:android=
  "http://schemas.android.com/apk/res/android"
    xmlns:tools="http://schemas.android.com/tools"
    android:layout_width="match_parent"
    android:layout_height="match_parent"
    android:paddingLeft="@dimen/activity_horizontal_margin"
android:paddingRight="@dimen/activity_horizontal_margin"
    android:paddingTop="@dimen/activity_vertical_margin"
    android:background="@android:color/holo_orange_dark"
    android:paddingBottom="@dimen/activity_vertical_margin"
    tools:context=".MainActivity">
  <ListView
      android:id="@+id/main_list"
      android:background="@android:color/holo_blue_bright"
      android:layout_width="match_parent"
      android:layout_height="match_parent"></ListView>
</RelativeLayout>
```

7. Create a new layout file and name it `adapter.xml`. Let's have some nested views and lots of background colors. All for the bad app:

```xml
<?xml version="1.0" encoding="utf-8"?>
<FrameLayout xmlns:android=
  "http://schemas.android.com/apk/res/android"
    android:orientation="vertical"
    android:layout_width="match_parent"
    android:background="@android:color/holo_green_light"
    android:padding="8dp"
    android:layout_height="match_parent">
  <ImageView
      android:id="@+id/main_image"
      android:src="@android:drawable/ic_media_play"
      android:layout_marginTop="8dp"
      android:layout_width="80dp"
      android:scaleType="fitCenter"
      android:layout_height="60dp" />
  <TableLayout
      android:layout_marginTop="8dp"
      android:layout_marginLeft="90dp"
      android:layout_width="match_parent"
      android:layout_height="wrap_content">
      <TableRow android:background=
        "@android:color/holo_purple">
          <TextView android:layout_width="match_parent"
              android:id="@+id/main_text_title"
```

```
                    android:layout_marginTop="8dp"
                    android:textSize="24sp"
                    android:layout_height="wrap_content"
                    android:textColor="@android:color/white"/>
        </TableRow>
            <TableRow android:background=
                "@android:color/holo_blue_light">
                <TextView android:layout_width="match_parent"
                    android:id="@+id/main_text_year"
                    android:layout_height="wrap_content"
                    android:textSize="20sp"
                    android:layout_marginTop="8dp"
                    android:textColor="@android:color/white"/>
        </TableRow>
            <TableRow android:background=
                "@android:color/holo_green_dark">
                <LinearLayout
                    android:orientation="vertical"
                    android:layout_height="wrap_content"
                    android:layout_width="match_parent"
                    android:layout_marginTop="16dp">
                    <TextView android:layout_width="match_parent"
                        android:id="@+id/main_text_genre"
                        android:layout_height="wrap_content"
                        android:textSize="16sp"
                        android:layout_marginTop="8dp"
                        android:background=
                          "@android:color/holo_green_dark"
                        android:textColor="@android:color/white"/>
                     <TextView android:layout_width="match_parent"
                        android:id="@+id/main_text_director"
                        android:layout_height="wrap_content"
                        android:textSize="16sp"
                        android:layout_marginTop="8dp"
                        android:background=
                          "@android:color/holo_green_light"
                        android:textColor="@android:color/white"/>
                    <TextView android:layout_width="match_parent"
                        android:id="@+id/main_text_actors"
                        android:layout_height="wrap_content"
                        android:textSize="16sp"
                        android:layout_marginTop="8dp"
                        android:background=
                          "@android:color/holo_green_dark"
                        android:textColor="@android:color/white"/>
                </LinearLayout>
            </TableRow>
        </TableLayout>
    </FrameLayout>
```

8. Open the `AndroidManifest.xml` file and add a permission for Internet access:

   ```
   <uses-permission android:name="android.permission.INTERNET" />
   ```

9. Create a new class and name it `BadMovie`:

   ```
   public class BadMovie {
       public String title;
       public String genre;
       public String year;
       public String director;
       public String actors;
       public String imageUrl;
       public BadMovie(String title, String genre, String
         year, String director, String actors, String
           imageUrl){
           this.title = title;
           this.genre = genre;
           this.year =year;
           this.director = director;
           this.actors = actors;
           this.imageUrl = imageUrl;
       }
   }
   ```

10. Create an adapter class and name it `MainAdapter`. We will be using a `ViewHolder` class, and we will create a separate thread to load each movie image from the Net:

    ```
    public class MainAdapter  extends ArrayAdapter<BadMovie> {
        private Context mContext;
        private int mAdapterResourceId;
        public List<BadMovie> Items = null;
        static class ViewHolder
            TextView title;
            TextView genre;
            ImageView image;
            TextView actors;
            TextView director;
            TextView year;
        }
        @Override
        public int getCount() {
            super.getCount();
            int count = Items != null ? Items.size() : 0;
            return count;
        }
        public MainAdapter(Context context, int adapterResourceId,
          List<BadMovie> items) {
            super(context, adapterResourceId, items);
            this.Items = items;
            this.mContext = context;
    ```

```
            this.mAdapterResourceId = adapterResourceId;
}
@Override
public View getView(int position, View convertView,
 ViewGroup parent) {
    View v = null;
    v = convertView;
    if (v == null) {

        LayoutInflater vi = (LayoutInflater)
        this.getContext().getSystemService(
         Context.LAYOUT_INFLATER_SERVICE);
        v = vi.inflate(mAdapterResourceId, null);
        ViewHolder holder = new ViewHolder();
        holder.title = (TextView) v.findViewById(
         R.id.main_text_title);
        holder.actors = (TextView) v.findViewById(
         R.id.main_text_actors);
        holder.image = (ImageView)
         v.findViewById(R.id.main_image);
        holder.genre = (TextView)
         v.findViewById(R.id.main_text_genre);
        holder.director = (TextView)
         v.findViewById(R.id.main_text_director);
        holder.year = (TextView)
         v.findViewById(R.id.main_text_year);
        v.setTag(holder);
    }

    final BadMovie item = Items.get(position);
    if (item != null) {
        final ViewHolder holder = (ViewHolder) v.getTag();
        holder.director.setText(item.director);
        holder.actors.setText(item.actors);
        holder.genre.setText(item.genre);
        holder.year.setText(item.year);
        holder.title.setText(item.title);
        new Thread(new Runnable() {
         public void run(){
           try {
             final Bitmap bitmap =
              BitmapFactory.decodeStream((
               InputStream) new
              URL(item.imageUrl).getContent());
             ((Activity)getContext()).runOnUiThread(new
             Runnable() {
```

```
            @Override
            public void run() {

                holder.image.setImageBitmap(bitmap);
              }
          });
        }
        catch (Exception e) {
          e.printStackTrace();
        }
      }
    }).start();;}
    return v;
  }
}
```

11. In the `MainActivity` file, add a private member that will contain all the movies:

```
private ArrayList<BadMovie> mBadMovies;
```

12. Add the implementation to the `onCreate` method to add a couple of thousand bad movies, creating an adapter for them and telling the list view about it:

```
mBadMovies = new ArrayList<BadMovie>();
for (int iRepeat=0;iRepeat<=20000;iRepeat++) {
    mBadMovies.add(new BadMovie("Popstar", "Comedy",
      "2000", "Paulo Segio de Almeida", "Xuxa Meneghel,
      Luighi Baricelli", "https://coversblog.files.
      wordpress.com/2009/03/xuxa-popstar.jpg"));
    mBadMovies.add(new BadMovie("Bimbos in Time", "Comedy",
      "1993", "Todd Sheets", "Jenny Admire, Deric Bernier",
      "http://i.ytimg.com/vi/bCHdQ1MB1D4/
      maxresdefault.jpg"));
    mBadMovies.add(new BadMovie("Chocolat", "Comedy",
      "2013", "Unknown", "Blue Cheng-Lung Lan, Masami
      Nagasawa", "http://i.ytimg.com/vi/EPlbiYD1MmM/
      maxresdefault.jpg"));
    mBadMovies.add(new BadMovie("La boda o la vida",
      "1974", "year", "Rafael Romero Marchent", "Manola
      Codeso, La Polaca", "http://monedasycolecciones.com/
      10655-thickbox_default/la-boda-o-la-vida.jpg"));
    mBadMovies.add(new BadMovie("Spudnuts", "Comedy",
      "2005", "Eric Hurt", "Brian Ashworth, Dave Brown,
      Mendy St. Ours", "http://lipponhomes.com/wp-
      content/uploads/2014/03/DSCN0461.jpg"));
}

//source: www.imdb.com
MainAdapter adapter = new MainAdapter(this,
  R.layout.adapter, mBadMovies);
((ListView)findViewById(R.id.main_list)).setAdapter(adapter);
```

13. Now run your app. According to the users at **Internet Movie Database** (**IMDB**), these are the worst comedy movies ever. We have added the movies many times on purpose to create a huge list where each row uses a primitive way of loading thumbnails from the Internet as shown in the following screenshot:

14. Depending on the device you are testing your app on, you need to scroll for a while or maybe the error appears right away.

15. This is what sooner or later appears in **LogCat**. Check the log after your app has crashed. Use the *Cmd + 6* shortcut (for Windows: *Alt +6*) to display **LogCat**. It will show you something like this:

```
packt.com.thebad E/AndroidRuntime: FATAL EXCEPTION: Thread-3529
java.lang.OutOfMemoryError: Failed to allocate a 7238412 byte
allocation with 53228 free bytes and 51KB until OOM
```

16. And here is where it happens:

```
At packt.com.thebad.MainAdapter$1.run(MainAdapter.java:82)
```

17. Have a look at the Memory and CPU Monitor as well. Your device is having a hard time. This is how it looks if you scroll through the list.

    The following screenshot provides the **Memory** report:

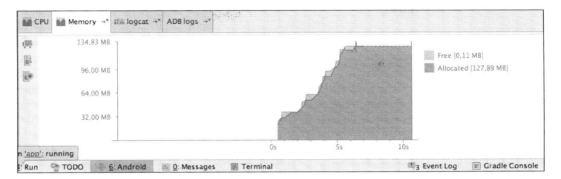

    The following screenshot provides the **CPU** report:

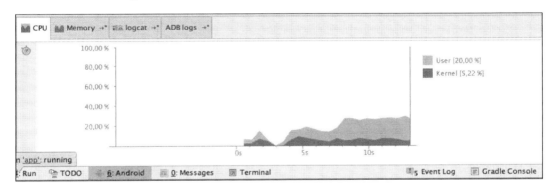

18. Well, this is what you get if you want to load full-size images multiple times. Since we are displaying thumbs anyway, there is not need for that and your device cannot handle it. Let's fix that.

 We are also having a threading issue as the wrong images may appear on the rows.

19. Although the best solution is to have a server return thumbnails instead of large images, we will not always be in the position to control that, in particular when dealing with third-party sources. So, one way to solve the memory issue is to set the `inSampleSize` property for `BitmapFactory Options` when loading the bitmap in the `MainAdapter` class, just like we did in the recipes of previous chapters.

20. However, it will be even more efficient to use the `Picasso` library here. `Picasso` is a popular image library that will simplify the process for us. Among other things, it will load an image from the Internet in a separate thread and will shrink it to the size of its container, here the image view in the adapter layout.

21. Open the `build.gradle` file in the `app` folder and add the dependency for `Picasso`:

```
dependencies {
    compile fileTree(dir: 'libs', include: ['*.jar'])
    compile 'com.squareup.picasso:picasso:2.3.3'
}
```

22. Save the file and click on the **Sync now** link that appears.

23. Open the `MainAdapter` class and replace the thread (and anything within it) that loads the image with just one line. Use the *Alt + Enter* shortcut to add the `Picasso` import:

```
Picasso.with(getContext()).load(item.imageUrl).resize(80,
    60).into(holder.image);
```

24. That is it. `Picasso` will take care of downloading and resizing the images.

25. Now run the app again and scroll through the list as much as you want. Both the memory and the threading problem have been solved. And the list view does scroll smoothly.

26. You will come to know what difference this makes if you have a look at both the **Memory** and the **CPU** tabs of the **Android** panel.

The following screenshot provides the **Memory** report:

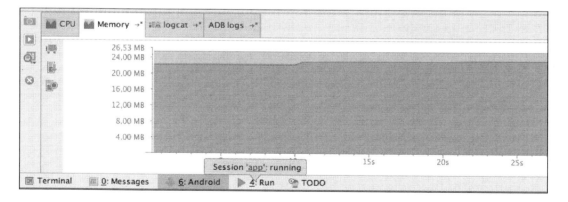

The following screenshot provides the **CPU** report:

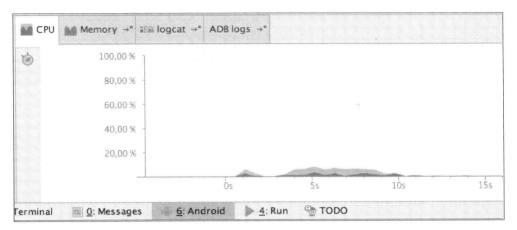

We just fixed our app, which is now capable of displaying a huge list of bad movies. In the next recipe, we will check whether we have any overdraw issues with the app. On older or less powerful devices, these issues may occur.

There's more...

`Picasso` also has some other interesting features such as creating round images, rotated images, or displaying error or placeholder images automatically.

An alternative to `Picasso` is the `Universal Image Loader` library.

`RetroFit` is a strongly recommended library for API communication. It is a REST client for Android and Java and it could save you a lot of time and headaches.

Android Studio tip

Want to refactor your code? Use the shortcut *Ctrl + T* (for Windows: *Ctrl + Alt + Shift + T*) to see what options you have. You can, for example, rename a class or method or extract code from a method.

Overdraw issues

The interface of your app needs to render quickly, and interaction, such as scrolling through a list, for example, should run smoothly. In particular, older or low-end devices often have a hard time to do these things right. An unresponsive or slow UI can be the result, which is often caused by something that is called overdraw.

Overdraw is the phenomenon of a pixel on a view being drawn more than once. A colored background with a view on top of that has another background color is an example of overdraw (the pixel is drawn twice), but that's not really an issue. Too much overdraw, however, will have an impact on your app's performance.

Getting ready

You will need to have a real device and you need to complete the `The Bad` app from the previous recipe to demonstrate overdraw issues, but you can examine any other app as well if you like.

How to do it...

Your device contains a couple of interesting developer options. One of them is the **Debug GPU overdraw** option which can be obtained by following next steps:

1. On your device, open the **Settings** app.
2. Select **Developer options**.

> If the **Developer options** item is not available on your device, you need to go to **About device** first and click seven times on **Build number**. Once you're done, go back. A new option called **Developer options** now appears in the list.

3. Find the **Debug GPU overdraw** option and click on it:

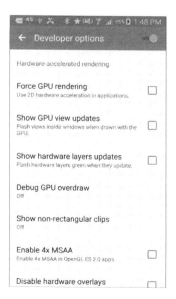

4. In the dialog that pops up, select the **Show overdraw** area.

5. Now, your device looks a little bit like a 3D movie without the corresponding glasses, but what actually is being shown here is this: colors indicate the amounts of overdraw, where no color means no overdraw (a pixel is painted only once), blue shows an overdraw of 1, green an overdraw of 2, light red an overdraw of 3, and dark red an overdraw of 4 times or even more.

 A maximum overdraw of 2 times is acceptable, so let's concentrate on the red sections.

6. Run the app you would like to examine. For this recipe, I have chosen to examine the `The Bad` app from the previous recipe, shown as follows:

7. Yeah, that is pretty bad. Every view has its own background color, resulting in overdraw.

8. Android is smart enough to reduce some overdraw cases, but for complex apps, you need to fix them yourself. When you look at the layout for both the activity and adapter from the previous recipe, this cannot be that difficult.

9. First, open the `activity_main.xml` layout file. Remove the `background` property from the list view, since it is not being used anyway. Also, remove the background property from the `RelativeLayout` file, as I do not like orange any way, at least not for apps.

10. Remove the `background` property from the `main_text_genre`, `main_text_director`, and the `main_text_actors` text views. Also, remove the `background` property from their parent view, which is the last `TableRow` appearing within `TableLayout`.

11. If you rerun the app, the app not only does the layout somewhat better, but you will also notice that there is less indication of overdraw.

12. Let's check whether we can make further improvements. Change `FrameLayout` at the root to `RelativeLayout`. Get rid of `TableLayout` and position the text views relatively:

```xml
<?xml version="1.0" encoding="utf-8"?>
<RelativeLayout xmlns:android=
  "http://schemas.android.com/apk/res/android"
    android:orientation="vertical"
    android:layout_width="match_parent"
    android:background="@android:color/holo_green_light"
    android:padding="8dp"
    android:layout_height="match_parent">
    <ImageView
        android:id="@+id/main_image"
        android:src="@android:drawable/ic_media_play"
        android:layout_marginTop="8dp"
        android:layout_width="80dp"
        android:scaleType="fitCenter"
        android:layout_height="60dp" />
    <TextView android:layout_width="match_parent"
        android:id="@+id/main_text_title"
        android:layout_marginTop="8dp"
        android:layout_toRightOf="@+id/main_image"
        android:background="@android:color/holo_purple"
        android:textSize="24sp"
        android:layout_height="wrap_content"
        android:textColor="@android:color/white"
        android:text="Line 1"/>
    <TextView android:layout_width="match_parent"
        android:id="@+id/main_text_year"
        android:layout_height="wrap_content"
        android:layout_toRightOf="@+id/main_image"
        android:layout_below="@+id/main_text_title"
        android:background=
```

```
            "@android:color/holo_blue_light"
        android:textSize="20sp"
        android:layout_marginTop="8dp"
        android:textColor="@android:color/white"
        android:text="Line 2"/>
    <TextView android:layout_width="match_parent"
        android:id="@+id/main_text_genre"
        android:layout_height="wrap_content"
        android:layout_toRightOf="@+id/main_image"
        android:layout_below="@+id/main_text_year"
        android:textSize="16sp"
        android:layout_marginTop="8dp"
        android:textColor="@android:color/white"
        android:text="Sub  1"/>
    <TextView android:layout_width="match_parent"
        android:id="@+id/main_text_director"
        android:layout_height="wrap_content"
        android:layout_toRightOf="@+id/main_image"
        android:layout_below="@+id/main_text_genre"
        android:textSize="16sp"
        android:layout_marginTop="8dp"
        android:textColor="@android:color/white"
        android:text="Sub 2"/>
    <TextView android:layout_width="match_parent"
        android:id="@+id/main_text_actors"
        android:layout_height="wrap_content"
        android:layout_toRightOf="@+id/main_image"
        android:layout_below="@+id/main_text_director"
        android:textSize="16sp"
        android:layout_marginTop="8dp"
        android:textColor="@android:color/white"
        android:text="Sub 3"/>
</RelativeLayout>
```

13. Run your app again. It is getting better and better, is it not?

14. To further improve your app, remove all `text` properties. They were only there to check whether we were doing the right thing using the `layout_toRightOf` and `layout_below` properties.

In this recipe, we have further improved our bad app by optimizing its layout. Also, it is no longer ugly. Actually, it has become quite good.

What layout type to use?

Using `RelativeLayout` is more effective than `LinearLayout` but unfortunately it is not so developer friendly if, for example, you want to move or remove a text view that another view is referring to using a relative property.

The `FrameLayout` is much less complex, but it does not have this problem, and it seems to perform as well as `RelativeLayout`.

On the other hand it is not intented to contain many child widgets. Please be aware that in the end what counts is the smallest number of nested layout views, so you should pick the container that suits your needs and performs best.

Awesome! Our app runs smoothly on all devices. We do not expect any weird errors any more.

Now let's ship it to our beta users to find out what they think of it. We will find out once we have completed the final chapter, where we will discuss *adhoc distribution*.

There's more...

There are more interesting tools that you perhaps would like to examine in order to improve the quality and performance of your app.

We have mentioned `Espresso` before. `Robotium` is another Android test automation framework for UI testing purposes. You can find it at `http://robotium.com`.

See also

- ▶ *Chapter 8, Improving Quality*
- ▶ *Chapter 10, Beta Testing Your App*

10

Beta Testing Your Apps

You did everything you could do to ensure the quality and performance of your app. Now it is time to ship your app to your beta users to see what they think of it.

Before shipping your app, you should have a look at Crashlytics first. You can find it at `https://try.crashlytics.com`.

Crashlytics can provide you with real-time crash reporting information not only during your beta tests, but also after releasing your app on the Play Store. Sooner or later, your app runs on a device that you have not tested your app on and it crashes on it. Crashlytics can help you find the cause for this.

Just download their SDK, add a few lines of code to your app, and you are good to go.

Distribute your app and get it tested before revealing your app to a large audience by publishing it on the Play Store. Learn from their feedback and improve your app.

At last, you can put this logo on your website:

In this chapter, you will learn about:

▶ Build variants

▶ Runtime permissions

▶ Play Store beta distribution

Introduction

A typical software release cycle goes like this, although it does not necessarily have to go through each phase:

Alpha -> closed beta -> open beta -> release.

You could release your app directly on the Google Play Store, but having at least one beta round is a clever thing to do. Gathering feedback and applying further improvements can make your app even better.

We will have a look at how to set up multiple different flavors for your app and how to define different build types for it. For example, your release app will most likely use different API endpoints than those you used to debug and test, at least I hope so.

The minimum API level you choose, the required features, and the requested permissions will affect the number of devices that your app will be available for in the Play Store. Also, we will have a preview of how runtime permissions that come with Android Marshmallow require a different approach.

Finally, we will find out what we need to do to distribute a beta or alpha version of our app using the Google Play Store.

Build variants

Android Studio supports different configurations for your app. For example, your app might use different API endpoints for debugging. For this purpose, we will use build types.

In addition to this, you may have different versions of your app. A single project can have multiple customized versions of the app. If these changes are minimal and, for example, just change the look of an app in case it is a white label solution using a flavor is the way to go.

A build variant is the combination of a build type and a particular flavor. The upcoming recipe will demonstrate how to use these.

Getting ready

For this recipe, you just need a recent copy of Android Studio.

How to do it...

We will build a simple messaging app that uses different build types and build flavors:

1. Create a new project in Android Studio, name it `WhiteLabelMessenger`, enter a company name in the **Company Domain** field, and click on the **OK** button.

2. Next, choose **Phone and Tablet** and click on the **Next** button.

3. Choose **Blank activity** and click on the **Next** button.

4. Accept the suggested values and click on the **Finish** button.

5. Open the `strings.xml` file and add a few extra strings. They should look like these:

```
<resources>
    <string name="app_name">WhiteLabelMessenger</string>
    <string name="hello_world">Hello world!</string>
    <string name="action_settings">Settings</string>
    <string name="button_send">SEND YEAH!</string>
    <string name="phone_number">Your phone number</string>
    <string name="yeah">Y-E-A-H</string>
    <string name="really_send_sms">YES</string>
</resources>
```

6. Create an `icon.xml` and a `background.xml` resource file in the `res/drawable` folder.

7. In the `res/drawable` folder, create a new file and name it `icon.xml`. It will draw a blue-colored circle:

```
<?xml version="1.0" encoding="utf-8"?>
<shape    xmlns:android="http://schemas.android.com/apk/res/
android"
    android:shape="oval">
    <solid
        android:color="@android:color/holo_blue_bright"/>
    <size
        android:width="120dp"
        android:height="120dp"/>
</shape>
```

8. In the `res/drawable` folder, create a new file and name it `background.xml`. It defines a gradient blue background:

```xml
<?xml version="1.0" encoding="utf-8"?>
<selector xmlns:android=
   "http://schemas.android.com/apk/res/android">
    <item>
        <shape>
            <gradient
                android:angle="90"
                android:startColor=
                 "@android:color/holo_blue_light"
                android:endColor=
                 "@android:color/holo_blue_bright"
                android:type="linear" />
        </shape>
    </item>
</selector>
```

9. Open the `activity_main.xml` file and modify it so that it looks like this:

```xml
<FrameLayout xmlns:android=
   "http://schemas.android.com/apk/res/android"
    xmlns:tools="http://schemas.android.com/tools"
     android:layout_width="match_parent"
     android:layout_height="match_parent"
     android:paddingLeft=
      "@dimen/activity_horizontal_margin"
     android:paddingRight=
      "@dimen/activity_horizontal_margin"
     android:paddingTop="@dimen/activity_vertical_margin"
     android:background="@drawable/background"
     android:paddingBottom=
      "@dimen/activity_vertical_margin"
     tools:context=".MainActivity">
    <EditText
        android:id="@+id/main_edit_phone_number"
        android:layout_marginTop="38dp"
        android:textSize="32sp"
        android:gravity="center"
        android:hint="@string/phone_number"
        android:layout_width="match_parent"
        android:layout_height="wrap_content" />
    <Button
        android:id="@+id/main_button_send"
        android:background="@drawable/icon"
        android:layout_gravity="center"
        android:layout_width="200dp"
        android:layout_height="200dp" />
```

```
<TextView
    android:text="@string/button_send"
    android:textSize="32sp"
    android:gravity="center"
    android:layout_gravity="bottom"
    android:textColor="@android:color/white"
    android:layout_width="match_parent"
    android:layout_height="wrap_content" />
</FrameLayout>
```

10. Open the `androidmanifest.xml` file and a permission to send SMS messages:

```
<uses-permission
  android:name="android.permission.SEND_SMS"/>
```

11. Modify the `onCreate` method of the `MainActivity` file. You can press *Shift* two times to display a search panel. Type `onCreate` on the search panel and select the `onCreate` method of the `MainActivity` class:

```
findViewById(R.id.main_button_send).setOnClickListener(this);
```

12. Add an on click listener on the `MainActivity` class and implement the `onClick` method:

```
public class MainActivity extends Activity implements View.
OnClickListener{
@Override
public void onClick(View v) {
    String phoneNumber = ((EditText)findViewById(
      R.id.main_edit_phone_number)).getText().toString();
    SmsManager sms = SmsManager.getDefault();
    String message = getString(R.string.yeah);
    if (getString(R.string.really_send_sms)  == "YES"){
     Toast.makeText(this, String.format(
       "TEST Send %s to %s", message, phoneNumber),
        Toast.LENGTH_SHORT).show();
    }
    else {
      sms.sendTextMessage(phoneNumber, null, message, null,
       null);

      Toast.makeText(this, String.format(
       "Send %s to %s",
        message, phoneNumber), Toast.LENGTH_SHORT).show();
    }
}
```

13. Select the `app` folder. Next, choose **Edit flavors** from the **Build** menu.

14. The list only contains a defaultConfig. Click on the **+** button to add a new flavor. Name it `blueFlavor` and give it the same values as `min sdk version` and `target sdk version` as is the case with **defaultConfig**.

15. For the **application id** field, use the package name **+** the extension `.blue`.

16. Enter the **version code** and **version name** for this flavor and click on the **OK** button.

17. Repeat step 14 to 16 for another flavor. Name that flavor `greenFlavor`.

18. Now your `build.gradle` file should contain the flavors as shown:

```
productFlavors {
    blueFlavor {
        minSdkVersion 21
        applicationId 'packt.com.whitelabelmessenger.blue'
        targetSdkVersion 21
        versionCode 1
        versionName '1.0'
    }
    greenFlavor {
        minSdkVersion 21
        applicationId 'packt.com.whitelabelmessenger.green'
        targetSdkVersion 21
        versionCode 1
        versionName '1.0'
    }
}
```

19. In the **Project** panel, select the `src` folder under the `app` folder. Then, create a new folder and name it `blueFlavor`. Within that folder, you can maintain the same structure, as is the case for the `main` folder. For this recipe, it is sufficient just to add a `res` folder and within that folder another one called `drawable`.

20. Do the same thing for the `greenFlavor` build's flavor. The project structure will now look like this:

21. Copy the `background.xml` and `icon.xml` files from the `/main/res/drawable` folder and paste them in the `blueFlavor/res/drawable` folder.

22. Repeat this for `greenFlavor` and open the `background.xml` file in the `greenFlavor/res/drawable` folder. Modify its content. For the green flavor, we will be using a gradient green color:

```xml
<?xml version="1.0" encoding="utf-8"?>
<selector xmlns:android=
  "http://schemas.android.com/apk/res/android">
    <item>
        <shape>
            <gradient
            android:angle="90"
            android:startColor=
              "@android:color/holo_green_light"
            android:endColor=
              "@android:color/holo_green_dark"
            android:type="linear" />
        </shape>
    </item>
</selector>
```

23. Now, within the same folder, open the `icon.xml` file and make the `drawable` folder appear in green as well:

```xml
<?xml version="1.0" encoding="utf-8"?>
<shape xmlns:android=
    "http://schemas.android.com/apk/res/android"
     android:shape="oval">
    <solid
        android:color="@android:color/holo_green_dark"/>
    <size
        android:width="120dp"
        android:height="120dp"/>
</shape>
```

24. The same thing can be done to use different values (or classes or layouts) for the debug and release build types. Create a `debug` folder in the `app/src` folder.

25. Within that folder, create a `res` folder and within that, a `values` folder.

26. Copy the `strings.xml` file from the `main/res/values` folder and paste it into the `debug/res/values` folder.

27. Open the `strings.xml` file and modify the `really_send_sms` string resource:

```xml
<string name="really_send_sms">NO</string>
```

 A better approach for this purpose of course will be to use a constants class that defines different values, but for the sake of simplicity, we will modify the string resource instead.

Build variants

Select the `app` folder and choose **Select Build Variant** from the **Build** menu. It will display the **Build variants** panel as shown in the following screenshot:

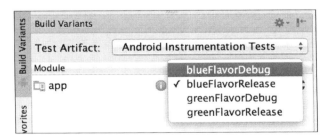

And follow the next steps in **Build Variants**:

1. Choose the **greenFlavorDebug** build variant and run the app.

2. If everything goes well, the app has a green look and behaves as if it is being debugged.

3. Now change the build variant to **blueFlavorDebug** and run the app again. Indeed, it looks blue now.

Build types

More or less the same thing applies to the debug and release build types; however, this time instead of the looks, the behavior or data (or end points for that matter) changes.

 Releasing the app requires signing, which is something we will do when we distribute the app to the Play Store, which has been described in the last recipe.

This is basically all there is to tell about build variants. Most ideal build types and flavors contain just a small number of modifications. If the differences between the various flavors of your app are more than just some tweaks in layouts, drawables, or constant values, you will have to consider a different approach.

There's more...

Android Studio comes with a couple of other great features to finalize your app. One of them is creating technical documentation automatically. Just add some comments to a class or method, like this:

```
/**
 * This is the main activity where all things are happening
 */
public class MainActivity extends Activity implements View.
OnClickListener{
```

Now if you choose **Generate JavaDoc** from the **Tools** menu and define the path in the **output directory** field in the dialog that appears, you just need to click the **OK** button and all documentation is being generated as HTML files. The outcome will be displayed in your browser as follows:

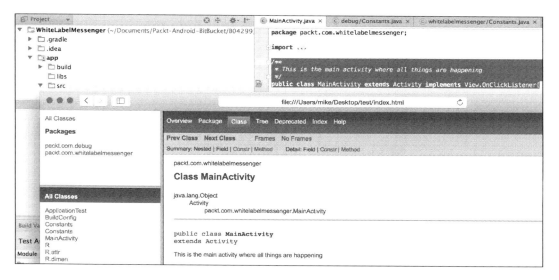

Android Studio tip

Do you often need to return to a particular place in your code? Create a bookmark with the *Cmd + F3* (for Windows: *F11*) shortcut.

To display a list of bookmarks and to choose from them, use the shortcut *Cmd + F3* (for Windows: *Shift + F11*).

Runtime permissions

The number of different types of devices that your app will target depends on the feature requirements (which needs permissions) and the markets at which you are targeting (by explicitly selecting specific countries or by offering your app in specific languages).

If, for example, your app requires both a front and a back camera, you will be targeting a smaller number of devices, as would be the case if you just require a back camera.

Usually when installing an app, the user is asked to accept (or decline) all the required permissions, as it has been defined in the `AndroidManifest` file of an app.

With the introduction of Android 6 (Marshmallow), the way a user is asked for particular permissions has changed. Only if a certain type of permission is required, the user will be prompted so that he can allow or deny that permission.

With that, there is an opportunity for the app to explain why this permission is needed. After this, the whole thing makes much more sense to the user. These so-called runtime permissions require a somewhat different development approach.

For this recipe, we will modify the previous app that sends SMSs. Now we need to ask the user's permission once he hits the button in order to send an SMS.

Getting ready

To test runtime permissions, you need to have a device running on Android 6.0 or higher or you need to have a virtual device running on Android Marshmallow or higher.

Also, make sure that you have downloaded the Android 6.x SDK (API Level 23 or above).

How to do it...

So, how do these runtime permissions look and how do we handle them? This can be checked with the help of the following steps:

1. Open the project from the previous recipe.

2. Open the `AndroidManifest` file and add the permission (according to the new model) to send **SMS** messages:

    ```
    <uses-permission-sdk-
     android:name="android.permission.SEND_SMS"/>
    ```

3. Open the `build.gradle` file in the `app` folder and set the value for `compileSdkVersion` to the latest available version. Also, change the values for each `minSdkVersion` and `targetSdkVersion` to 23 or above.

4. Modify the `onClick` method:

    ```
    @Override
    public void onClick(View v) {
        String phoneNumber = ((EditText) findViewById(
         R.id.main_edit_phone_number)).getText().toString();
        String message = getString(R.string.yeah);
        if (Constants.isTestSMS) {
          Toast.makeText(this, String.format(
            "TEST Send %s to %s", message, phoneNumber),
            Toast.LENGTH_SHORT).show();
        }
        else {
          if (checkSelfPermission(Manifest.permission.SEND_SMS)
            != PackageManager.PERMISSION_GRANTED) {
                requestPermissions(new String[]{

                  Manifest.permission.SEND_SMS},
                    REQUEST_PERMISSION_SEND_SMS);
          }
        }
    }
    ```

5. Add a constant value so that later we will know to which permission request the permission result is referring to:

    ```
    private final int REQUEST_PERMISSION_SEND_SMS = 1;
    ```

6. Implement the `sendSms` method. We will use the `SmsManager` method to send the Y-E-A-H text to the phone number that the user has entered. Once the message has been sent, a toast will be displayed:

    ```
    private void sendSms(){
        String phoneNumber = ((EditText) findViewById(
    ```

```
        R.id.main_edit_phone_number)).getText().toString();
    String message = getString(R.string.yeah);
    SmsManager sms = SmsManager.getDefault();
    sms.sendTextMessage(phoneNumber, null,
      getString(R.string.yeah), null, null);
    Toast.makeText(this, String.format("Send %s to %s",
      getString(R.string.yeah), phoneNumber),
       Toast.LENGTH_SHORT).show();
}
```

7. Finally, implement the `onRequestPermissionsResult` method. If the granted permission is the permission for an SMS, then call the `sendSms` method. If the permission is denied, a toast will be displayed and the **send** button and the edit text to enter the phone number will be disabled:

```
@Override
public void onRequestPermissionsResult(int requestCode,  String
permissions[], int[] grantResults) {
    switch (requestCode) {
        case REQUEST_PERMISSION_SEND_SMS: {
            if (grantResults[0] ==
              PackageManager.PERMISSION_GRANTED) {
                sendSms();
            }
            else {
              findViewById(
                R.id.main_edit_phone_number).setEnabled(
                  false);
              findViewById(
                R.id.main_button_send).setEnabled( false);
                Toast.makeText(this,
                  getString(R.string.no_sms_permission),
                   Toast.LENGTH_SHORT).show();
            }
            return;
        }
    }
}
```

8. Run your app. Use a device running on Android 6.0 or higher or create a virtual device that runs on the API level 23 or above.

9. Now the permission to send the SMS will not be asked upfront (that is, if the user installs the application). Instead, a dialog asking for permission pops up as soon as you hit the **Send** button.

10. If you agree with the request permission, the SMS message will be sent. If you deny the requested permission, the edit box and the button will be disabled and a toast will be displayed to provide feedback:

This recipe has demonstrated the basic idea of runtime permissions.

There's more...

To see how and when to ask for permission, or how and when to provide feedback about particular features that are not available, you can check the Google guidelines at https://www.google.com/design/spec/patterns/permissions.html.

> **Android Studio tip**
>
> You can easily extract code from a method that has become too large. Just mark the code that you want to move and use the shortcut *Cmd + Alt + M* (for Windows: *Ctrl + Alt + M*).

Play Store beta distribution

All right, we are going to upload our app to the Play Store as a beta distribution. Exciting, isn't it?

Getting ready

For this recipe, we will be using the app from the first recipe; although, any app that you consider to be ready for the beta launch will do.

Make sure you do have some artwork for it as well, such as icons and screenshots. Don't worry, for this recipe, you can download these items as well from <www.packtpub.com>. Also, think about your app's metadata, such as title, description, and category.

Most important is that you do have a developers account and that you do have access to the Google Play Developer console. If you do not have an account, you need to register first via http://developer.android.com/distribute/googleplay/start.html.

How to do it...

Getting your app into the Play Store is not so hard. It just takes some time to set up things the right way:

1. Sign in to your **Google Play Developer Console** webpage or register first if you need to.
2. On the dashboard, click on the **Add new application** button.
3. In the dialog, enter the **Title** of the application `Blue Messenger` and click on the **Upload now APK** button.
4. You will notice the **production, beta**, and **alpha** tabs. Ideally, you start with alpha testing, but for demonstration purposes, we will choose the **beta** tab right away. On that, the **Upload your first APK to beta** button is shown. Click on that button.
5. In Android Studio, open the app that we created for the first (or second) recipe and from the **Build** menu, choose the **Generate signed APK** option.
6. Select the `app` module and click on the **Next** button.

7. Enter the **path** to your key store. If you do have one, click on the **Create new...** button and find a good place for your key store file (with the .jks extension). Enter a **password** for it, repeat the password, and enter a suitable value for **First and last name**. Then, click on the **OK** button.

8. Enter the **key store password**, create a new **key alias**, and name it whitelabelmessenger. Enter a **password** for the key and click on the **Next** button.

9. Enter the **master password** if needed and click on the **OK** button.

10. Modify the **destination path** if you wish and then select a **build type** and **flavor**. Choose **release** and **blueFlavor** and then click on the **OK** button.

11. A new dialog informs us that a new-signed APK has been created successfully if everything goes well. Click on the **Reveal in Finder** (or find it using Windows Explorer in case you are using Windows) button to see the APK file that has just been created.

12. In your browser, upload this APK file. Once the APK file has been uploaded, the version is displayed on the **beta** tab; you can pick a testing method and you see the number of supported devices, which will depend on the API level you have chosen and the required feature that comes with the SMS permission (which will exclude many tablets right away for example).

13. For the testing method, click on the **Setup closed beta testing** button.

14. Create a list by clicking on the **Create a list** button. Give the list a name, for example, **Internal testing** and add the e-mail addresses of the testers (or just for practicing purpose, enter your own). When you are done, click on the **Save** button.

15. Enter your own e-mail address as **Feedback channel** and click on the **Save draft** button.

16. Although we are not publishing anything on the store yet, you need to enter some values for the **Store listing** section, which is an option that you can select from the menu on the left-hand side of the webpage:

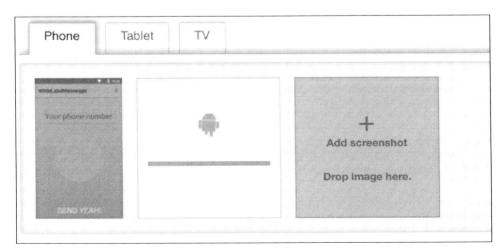

17. Enter title, short, and long description. Also, add two screenshots, a high-resolution icon and a feature graphic image. You can download these resources from `<www.packtpub.com>` or you can create them yourself by capturing screenshots from your app and have some fun with some kind of a paint program to give them the right widths and heights.

18. At **categorization**, choose **applications** as the **application type** and **Social** or **Communication** as the **category**.

19. Enter your **contact details** and select **Not submitting a privacy policy at this time** (unless you do want to do so, of course).

20. Click on the **Save draft** button and continue with the **Content Rating** section by choosing this option from the menu on the left-hand side of the screen.

Rate your app

Click on the **Continue** button, enter your **e-mail address**, and answer the questions about whether your app has any violent, sexual, or other potential dangerous content or features. Finally, click on the **Save Questionnaire** button:

1. You may now click on the **Calculate Rating** button. Your rating will be displayed after that. Click on the **Apply Rating** button and you are done.

2. The next section is **Pricing and Distribution**. Pick this option from the **menu** on the left-hand side of the page.

3. Make it a free app by clicking on the **Free** button and **choose to select all countries** (or specify specific countries if you wish). After that, click on the **Save Draft** button.

4. By now, the **Publish app** button should be enabled. Click on it. If it is not enabled, you can click on the **I can't publish?** link to find out what information is missing.

5. Here, the term "publishing" is a bit confusing. It actually means, in this context, that the app will be published for the test users that are on the list that you just created. Do not worry. Until you promote the app to production, nothing will be available at the Play Store, although the term "publishing" seems to suggest this.

6. While your app status says **Pending publication**, you can investigate some other options such as the list of devices your app is supporting, the required features, and permissions and options for analytical purposes, including features split testing (A/B tests).

Have a break

The **Pending publication** status may take a couple of hours (or perhaps even longer) as recently (since April 2015) Google announced that it will be reviewing the apps upfront (in a half-manual-half-automated way) even for alpha and beta distributions.

1. Eat a marshmallow or have some coffee or have a walk in the park. Return within a couple of hours to check whether your app's status has changed to **Published**. It may take some time, but it will.

 Your testers might need to change their (security) settings to **allow to install apps outside of Google Play Store**.

2. There are some other things that look confusing. Behind the package name, there will be a link that reads **View in Play Store...** and a hint saying that alpha and beta apps are not listed in the Play Store.

3. Click on the **APK** item in the menu on the left-hand side of the webpage. By following the link, you will find **Opt In Url** on the **Beta** tab that your test users can download and use to install the beta app:

Blue Messenger
Finiware

Finiware has invited you to a testing program for an unreleased version of **Blue Messenger**.

As a tester, you'll receive an update that includes a beta version of **Blue Messenger**. Please note that beta versions may be unstable or have a few bugs.

Send your feedback to **Finiware** using the contact information: **mike.van.drongelen@**

BECOME A BETA TESTER

Huge! Your first beta distribution is ready to be tested. You might need multiple iterations to get things right or maybe just one beta version will turn out to be sufficient to find out that your app is ready for the **Play Store**.

To release your app on the Play Store, click on the **Promote to Prod** button, if you dare...

And with that, this book ends. There is so much more to tell and to learn about Android development, such as services, Android Pay, **Near Field Communication** (**NFC**), and Bluetooth to name just a few; however, by reading this book, you have seen most of the elements of the Android Studio IDE and that was what we were aiming at.

So this is it for now. Thank you for reading, and happy coding!

There's more...

You should be aware of the fact that besides technology, methodology will be just as important. It is hard to develop an app that is not only technically perfect but also has a lot of users who are so happy with your app and its flow, usability, and appearance that they all give you the five stars that you deserve.

I assume you do not want to develop an app for months or for years only to find out later that actually nobody cares about it. To find out at an early stage what makes people really want to use your app, you should consider the lean start-up methodology for your app development.

Build – Measure – Learn

The **lean start-up** methodology is a method to develop businesses and products (or services). The idea is that experiments based on hypotheses, validated learning, and iterative product releases lead to shorter product development cycles.

Most important key elements of the lean start-up methodology are:

- **Minimum viable product** (**MVP**)
- Split testing and actionable metrics
- Continuous deployment

In short, a MVP is a version of a product that takes minimal effort to test particular ypotheses.

To learn more about the Lean start-up methodologies, check out the website `http://theleanstartup.com`, read Eric Ries' book, or find a lean start-up event near you from `http://www.leanstartupcircle.com`.

The **Play Store developer console** provides options for split testing and to measure how your app is being used. Google analytics can help you to do this as it is the easiest way to get actionable metrics, which you will need to gather for feedback in order to improve your app by learning from it.

Continuous deployment nicely fits into the Lean Start-up methodology. It can improve the quality and speed of your app development.

You might wonder what continuous deployment is about. It takes another book to fully explain the concept, but here is a short introduction to continuous integration and continuous delivery, which, if combined, is what continuous deployment is about.

Continuous integration (**CI**) is the process where developers commit their changes and merge results to a source code repository. A build server observes the code repository for changes, pulling and compiling code. The server also runs automated tests.

Continuous delivery is the process of creating deployable versions of your app automatically, for example, by publishing an alpha or beta app in the Play Store. For this reason, it is important that the submitted and validated code will be in an always-deployable state.

Setting up continuous deployment will take some upfront, but in the end, it will result in smaller and faster development cycles.

For a continuous deployment of your Android app, both `Jenkins` and `TeamCity` will be suitable. `Teamcity` is recommended most often and does integrate with Android Studio using a plugin.

To learn how to set up a `TeamCity` server or to find any further information, you can check the website of Packt Publishing that offers some great books that explain the concept of continuous integration and `TeamCity` in particular.

Index

A

Android Marshmallow (6.0) 3
Android Studio
  about 2
  fragmentation 2-4
  URL 2
Android Wear 61, 62
annotations
  about 145
  URL 158
app
  communicating with, content
      providers used 138-141
  Hello Android studio app, creating 4-7
  performance improvements 175-185
  testing, with Genymotion emulator 9-13

B

Behavior-driven Development (BDD) 162
build types 199-201
build variants 192-198

C

Calabash
  about 162, 163
  URL 163
card views
  about 39-44
  using 44-46
cloud
  data, consuming from 22-27
  data, submitting 28-35
code
  refactoring 13-15

code analysis 164-167
content providers
  about 118
  design patterns 118
  loader manager 127-132
  query method, implementing 122-127
  RxJava 118
  used, for communicating with
      other apps 138-141
  used, for consuming data 119-122
  used, for updating data 119-122
context stream 72
continuous delivery 210
continuous deployment 209
continuous integration (CI) 209
Crashlytics
  URL 191
Cucumber
  about 162, 163
  URL 163

D

Dalvik Debug Monitor Server (DDMS) 172
data
  consuming, content providers used 119-122
  consuming, from cloud 22-27
  submitting, to cloud 28-35
  updating, content providers used 119-122
devices 77
Domain-specific Language (DSL) 8
Do not Repeat Yourself (DRY) 144

E

elevations 46-53
Espresso 162

Thank you for buying
Android Studio Cookbook

About Packt Publishing

Packt, pronounced 'packed', published its first book, *Mastering phpMyAdmin for Effective MySQL Management*, in April 2004, and subsequently continued to specialize in publishing highly focused books on specific technologies and solutions.

Our books and publications share the experiences of your fellow IT professionals in adapting and customizing today's systems, applications, and frameworks. Our solution-based books give you the knowledge and power to customize the software and technologies you're using to get the job done. Packt books are more specific and less general than the IT books you have seen in the past. Our unique business model allows us to bring you more focused information, giving you more of what you need to know, and less of what you don't.

Packt is a modern yet unique publishing company that focuses on producing quality, cutting-edge books for communities of developers, administrators, and newbies alike. For more information, please visit our website at www.packtpub.com.

About Packt Open Source

In 2010, Packt launched two new brands, Packt Open Source and Packt Enterprise, in order to continue its focus on specialization. This book is part of the Packt open source brand, home to books published on software built around open source licenses, and offering information to anybody from advanced developers to budding web designers. The Open Source brand also runs Packt's open source Royalty Scheme, by which Packt gives a royalty to each open source project about whose software a book is sold.

Writing for Packt

We welcome all inquiries from people who are interested in authoring. Book proposals should be sent to author@packtpub.com. If your book idea is still at an early stage and you would like to discuss it first before writing a formal book proposal, then please contact us; one of our commissioning editors will get in touch with you.

We're not just looking for published authors; if you have strong technical skills but no writing experience, our experienced editors can help you develop a writing career, or simply get some additional reward for your expertise.

Android Native Development Kit Cookbook

ISBN: 978-1-84969-150-5   Paperback: 346 pages

A step-by-step tutorial with more then 60 concise recipes on Android NDK development skills

1. Build, debug, and profile Android NDK apps.

2. Implement part of Android apps in native C/C++ code.

3. Optimize code performance in assembly with Android NDK.

Android 3.0 Application Development Cookbook

ISBN: 978-1-84951-294-7   Paperback: 272 pages

Over 70 working recipes covering every aspect of Android development

1. Written for Android 3.0 but also applicable to lower versions.

2. Quickly develop applications that take advantage of the very latest mobile technologies, including web apps, sensors, and touch screens.

3. Part of Packt's Cookbook series: Discover tips and tricks for varied and imaginative uses of the latest Android features.

Please check **www.PacktPub.com** for information on our titles

Android User Interface Development Beginner's Guide

ISBN: 978-1-84951-448-4   Paperback: 304 pages

Quickly design and develop compelling user interfaces for your Android applications

1. Leverage the Android platform's flexibility and power to design impactful user-interfaces.

2. Build compelling, user-friendly applications that will look great on any Android device.

3. Make your application stand out from the rest with styles and themes.

Android 4: New Features for Application Development

ISBN: 978-1-84951-952-6   Paperback: 166 pages

Develop Android applications using the new features of Android Ice Cream Sandwich

1. Learn new APIs in Android 4.

2. Get familiar with the best practices in developing Android applications.

3. Step-by-step approach with clearly explained sample codes.

Please check **www.PacktPub.com** for information on our titles